LOVE'S TRIUMPH

With love and all of God's blessings!
Patsy

LOVE'S TRIUMPH

Dr. Patricia Kentz

Copyright © 2012 by Patricia Kentz
Cover design by Cory Sea

ISBN 978-0-7414-7311-0 Paperback
ISBN 978-0-7414-7312-7 eBook

Printed in the United States of America

Published November 2012

INFINITY PUBLISHING

Toll-free (877) BUY BOOK
Local Phone (610) 941-9999
Fax (610) 941-9959
Info@buybooksontheweb.com
www.buybooksontheweb.com

This book is dedicated
with love
to my husband,
Jim.

ACKNOWLEDGEMENTS

It never occurred to me to write a book. Even if it had, I would never have believed I could do it. It was my sister, Maryanne, who encouraged me and then stayed by my side every step of the way.

It has been good for me to write my story. Almost all of us in recovery have remorse about what alcoholism has done to our lives and the lives of those we love. By telling my story, I believe I can put the past behind me and embrace my recovery with even greater appreciation and joy.

Truth be told, love has triumphed in my life. So writing this story does not simply relieve me. It also acknowledges all those who have loved me, sometimes against all odds, in my long journey to sobriety.

I particularly would like to thank my friends who have supported me so fully, including my long-time and devoted friend, Carol, my cousin and art teacher, Jody and my dear friend, Marialice.

I would like to acknowledge the support of my brothers, Rick and Andrew and their wives, Lynn and Ellen, over the years.

I also would like to thank my brother-in-law, Cory, a wonderful artist and musician, who created the design for the book cover and gave me my first website.

During my time in Alcoholics Anonymous, I have had several sponsors who have tirelessly supported me, including Margaret, who has recently died, and my current sponsor, Ellen.

My parents, Rita and Fred Kentz, demonstrated an incredible love for me, despite the many and severe challenges that my alcoholism brought into their lives.

From the time I was very young, I have always described my sister, Maryanne, as my "favorite sister." Of course, I have only one sister. However, I could never have asked for a better one!

Finally, I thank my husband, Jim, for the boundless love that he has given me for over twenty years. His steadfast devotion and support of every kind have transformed my life.

Please note that several names and identifying characteristics have been changed in this book so as to provide certain individuals with complete anonymity. Also, I have not listed all the rehabilitation centers where I stayed during my long journey to sobriety as it would have rendered the book tedious to read. Suffice it to say that I did spend considerably longer time in rehab than most people do. The words of one of my loyal dental patients describes my journey well, "Oh, I'll just have to catch her between rehabs!"

CHAPTER ONE

On the outside, my life was picture perfect. I grew up in Summit, New Jersey with rolling hills, tall oak trees, each home more beautiful than the next. Our home was a magnificent, seven bedroom English tudor on a half acre of manicured lawns. In the spring, the azaleas and daffodils would take your breath away. Our home, 239 Oak Ridge Avenue, was listed in Home and Garden Magazine, and as one of Jackie Kennedy's ten favorite homes in the United States.

I was the third of four children, born less than six years apart. We were not only close in age, but close to each other emotionally.

Maryanne is the oldest child and my only sister. She was my best friend. In youth, she had curly auburn hair, lots of freckles and hazel eyes. In contrast, I had long straight blonde hair, the olive skin of my father and bright blue eyes. When we stood next to each other, no one would have ever guessed we were sisters. When I was with Maryanne, I felt safe.

My brother, Rick, is the oldest boy and Andrew is the "baby" being two years younger than I.

In childhood, Rick had blonde hair and blue eyes like me. Andrew had reddish hair and freckles like Maryanne. Rick was serious and Andrew was carefree. They could not have been more different, yet they were still close to each other.

Both my mother and father were responsible for this closeness. Born into a large Irish Catholic family, Mom knew the joyous and loving support of her many brothers and sisters. She did not force any closeness upon us children. She simply invited it to develop naturally as it had in her home many years before.

Dad was an only child but surrounded by three maiden aunts and one uncle who loved him as if he were their own. In addition, he had four cousins, all girls. They all lived in the same town so he too knew the joy of a large family.

Together my parents encouraged a deep connection between us that surpassed any differences in looks or personalities. When I was with my sister and brothers, I relaxed and felt safe. When I was alone, my world was not the same at all.

Mom told me that I was a "lost child." I think she was right. I remember looking in the mirror often, trying to figure out if I was pretty or special in some way. I remember being in my room and studying as hard as I could, hoping to excel in some spectacular way. I remember watching Maryanne talk so much and excitedly about everything, and wondering how I could ever match the way she made herself seen and heard. All of these efforts were futile. The bottom line was that I did not believe I had much worth and everything I tried in order to change this did not work.

Really, it could not have been any other way. Mom waited five years before Maryanne arrived. Five long, painful years while all her friends had already become mothers. When Maryanne finally arrived, she was the focus

of my parents' lives. At dinner they put Marya[...]
basket on the dining room table. One would take a [...]
food while the other entertained Maryanne, then the o[...]
would take a bite. She was their world.

Rick arrived just thirteen months after Maryanne and
my parents' focus widened to include their first son. By the
time I arrived, however, their lives were already too full
with two toddlers to make a lot of room for me, or so Mom
told me.

Of course, I did not make it easy for them to find me. I
was very placid to the point of being completely non-
demanding. I was quiet, very much so compared to
Maryanne, who was a chatterbox. I was compliant
compared to Rick, who was strong and forceful. And, of
course, I was not "the baby." So I assumed the stereotypical
role of the third child quite naturally.

Mom sensed this happening. She told me stories years
later that confirmed her sense of things. Once she told me
that she was so exhausted from taking care of Maryanne and
Rick, who had been very sick with the flu for a week, that
when I approached and saying that I did not feel well, she
replied, "Oh no, not you too, Patsy. I am so tired. I just can't
have one more sick child."

I accepted her words without complaint. It did not
occur to me whine, cry or have a tantrum. The next day I
went up to her and asked if it was okay to be sick that day.
She also said that a few years later on my first day of
nursery school, she watched me go out the door and she
cried all day. When I returned home that afternoon I asked
her why she was crying. She said, "I just don't know you,
Patsy. Somehow you got lost." So I spent much of my early
childhood wanting to be seen and wanting to be special, but

ıg up when I sensed that neither was

ɔgan to recognize these feelings of
see they often became more intense
ɔf my father or even when I thought of

However, It took me years to realize that Dad and I were remarkably alike and that this was a part of our challenge together. He was stubborn and determined just as I am. His determination was evident right from birth just as mine was. His mother suffered many miscarriages before she gave birth to him, who was the only child. And after I was born, the pediatrician told Mom that I had quite a prominent jaw, which he said gave me a solidly determined look right from the first day of my life.

I believe Dad recognized this similarity. In fact, I sensed he saw a reflection of himself in me: the same ruthless determination, the same defiance and most of all, the same pain. Despite the public prominence that his position as lawyer and judge bestowed, I believe Dad was just as insecure as I was.

Despite the similarities, there was, of course, one difference. He was my father and I was his child. I wanted to relax and feel supported by him, but this was difficult from a very early age. Over time, and in many moments, it became impossible.

I am certain that Dad did not know how to handle this reflection of himself. No doubt he wanted to keep his heart open to me, but he simply could not in many moments. He became remarkably aloof, not wanting to know much about my life or me. Sometimes he was unkind and heartlessly insensitive. He yelled endlessly at times, or so it seemed to me.

I first remember feeling Dad's anger when I was three. It was a Sunday morning and Maryanne, who was 7, was dressing me for Church. As she bent over to buckle my patent leather shoes, Dad charged into the room yelling at us to hurry or we would be late for Church. The yelling continued as Maryanne tried to quickly finish my shoes and find my coat and hat. I remember seeing her stiffened body rushing around the room, desperate to get me out the door. I did not like the yelling either and I too stiffened in fear. But there was a difference. I was determined that Dad would not see my fear. Even at this young age I was determined to prove that no matter what he did or said, it did not bother me. It would take many years to acknowledge that just the opposite was true.

When I was 6, I had my first taste of Dad's response to a task not performed to his satisfaction. I set the dinner table by myself for the first time. When I finished, I sat in one of the chairs and eyed my accomplishment with pride. Dad walked into the room a few moments later and began yelling uncontrollably because I placed a spoon in the wrong place. I remember the exact moment when I felt like collapsing but made myself hold on, determined again to prove that his anger did not hurt me.

I am sure Maryanne sensed my pain. Why else would she regularly sneak into my room in the middle of the night and carry me back into her bed? Why else would she set her old-fashioned wind up alarm clock to go off an hour before Dad's, place it under her pillow so it would not be heard, allowing her to get me back into bed before he awoke?

I continued to protect myself in my own way, too. I simply refused to acknowledge any pain. When Dad asked how Maryanne's day at school had been but did not ask about mine, I held myself tight on the inside but appeared cool on the outside. Though all the while, I was plodding my pathway. The pathway I hoped would guarantee Dad's appreciation, approval and love for me. It was a pathway I would not veer from for years to come.

CHAPTER TWO

ACHIEVEMENT became my singular pathway. I seized every opportunity for achievement at school as well as at home. This was not difficult at school as it was one that offered children an abundance of opportunities for excellence, in addition to many opportunities for relaxation and enjoying life.

I loved Oak Knoll School of the Holy Child, which I attended from the time I was six to the time I was eighteen. Unlike Catholic parochial schools, Oak Knoll was a private school run by the nuns of the Society of the Holy Child. The nuns had a mission: to impart the love of God in all their activities with us, their students. The motto of the Society of the Holy Child was "Actions, not words." Living their motto, the nuns at Oak Knoll inspired us not through speech or rhetoric but rather through their own example of a life of simple happiness in God.

Fulfilling their mission was a tall order, but the nuns succeeded over and over to the point that Oak Knoll was a profoundly unique school.

The kindergarten was unlike any other. Two tall brass aviaries were at one end of the room and housed all manners of birds, including several large white cockatoos. Beyond the cockatoos one could see out through the glass doors to a virtual forest of oak trees, leaving a multitude of acorns for us to tromp on at recess.

There was a shiny mahogany piano on which our teacher played Beethoven's Minuet in G while we, as gracefully as six-year-olds could, danced in time with our partners. No detail was spared in bringing music, nature and beauty together to create a place of order, serenity and happiness in our kindergarten.

I guess this is why the accident came as such a surprise as it happened on a day when the kindergarten seemed especially sublime. It was our Christmas party day, held on the last day prior to our Christmas break, and the room was resplendent with tiny white lights glowing from two large spruce Christmas trees.

I arrived in my best white party dress with its petticoat expanded to God knows where. My straight hair, studiously transformed by my mother into a cascade of curls, was held in place by bright pink bows. When Mom said I was pretty as a picture, I looked in the mirror and agreed. I could not wait for all my friends to see me.

But the friends had no time to notice the curls, the ribbons or billowing petticoat. Within minutes of arriving, I tripped while playing Ring Around the Rosie and my jaw crashed hard onto the marble floor. The pink bows quickly became crimson red as blood saturated them and my dress. As I lay on the floor with everything swirling around me, I wondered how joy could vanish so quickly.

Mom was at home when the school notified her. Maryanne, who was in the fourth grade, was also called to the scene. Maryanne, of course, arrived first. I knew her voice so well and could hear her arguing with the janitor, who was trying to move a large potted orange tree through the hallway, which was blocking her way. She told him to move the orange tree immediately and surprisingly, he did.

She pushed her way through the people to find me, and held me in her arms. She told me that everything would be fine. My white party dress was soaked in blood. I did not know what happened, but knew that everything would be fine because Maryanne was with me. I had a large gash on my chin that required fourteen stitches. The scar never went away, but neither did the feeling of being so loved.

When inside the walls of Oak Knoll, I often felt loved and protected, but I also felt inspired. In feeling the nuns surrender in happiness to God, I was inspired to make the same gesture.

Our daily life at Oak Knoll encouraged this devotion. Every day we walked down the long corridor from the kindergarten to the chapel, girls on one side and boys on the other. Eyes downward, we fastened ourselves to a thin gold line on the green marble floor so we did not lose our balance and crash into the next student. Once we entered the chapel, however, my eyes could do nothing more than gaze at the beauty of white brightness of this holy sanctuary. Everything in the chapel was a creamy white – the statues, the walls, the small louvered shutters. This seemed to serve as a reminder that no matter what we were feeling, there was nothing but beautiful white light.

I am sure this wonderful feeling of being transported did not happen to everyone everyday. But it happened to me and it happened often. My life would never have been the same without it.

While daily life at Oak Knoll focused on and expanded from these times in the chapel, there was also an experience once a year that was unforgettable.

It was the Oak Knoll Christmas pageant.

The auditorium was large enough to hold about four hundred people. Every year well over four hundred parents, grandparents and friends squeezed themselves in to see the pageant, a miraculous product of months of focus by nuns and children alike.

Miraculous indeed as every student, regardless of age, maintained complete composure for over two hours. No legs were crossed, no shoulders hunched, not one whisper uttered. Every child knew this was a sacred time and wanted to honor it.

In front of the red velvet curtained stage sat the high school glee club on one side, and the younger, less vocally adept on the other. We sat perched on bleachers so that every parent and grandparent in the audience could see his special charge. We wore white dresses and royal blue sashes with a sprig of holly dutifully pinned on the right side of the dress by one of the nuns.

The students were under the musical direction of Mr. G. Marston Haddock, a man whose passion belied his reserved English background. Mr. Haddock had a singular passion: that Oak Knoll singing be exquisite. Though he toiled tirelessly for every Oak Knoll occasion, this cold night right before Christmas every year was most important to him. For on this night, G. Marston Haddock wanted all to know through the power of voices uplifted, that the Divine was truly alive in our midst. So when Mr. Haddock leaned forward in his high chair to the point that he almost fell off, we did the same, leaning into the passion that he invited and feeling transported ourselves.

In the moments when we were not singing, the power of visual beauty caused many in the audience to gasp. Even those seasoned parents who attended the pageant every year, like mine, were affected.

When the red velvet curtains opened, there in stark relief was a scene from the Nativity. Whether it was the shepherds watching their flocks or the three Kings arriving in Bethlehem. It did not matter. One scene was as beautiful as the next – each resplendent with children dressed in handmade costumes sewn with gold thread, and each holding complete attention for every second that the curtains were opened.

No one on stage ever uttered a word. After all, these were "tableaux", the French word for pictures, and no words were needed. Each child's complete attention conveyed the communication of the heavenly.

Maryanne and I were never chosen to be on stage, but that did not matter. We sang with all our hearts, and rested in the sense that what was happening was greater than our own preferences. Heavenly as the performance was each year, there was inevitably a touch of the earthly, a reminder that this is an imperfect realm.

FALL ON YOUR KNEES!

When the majestic lines from "O, Holy Night" were sung, the more vocally skilled glee club joined together in song with the rest of the student body. To make the moment even more dramatic, we were instructed that we must all stand together at exactly the same moment, despite how discordant it seemed to be singing "Fall on Your Knees" while leaping to our feet!

So, leap we did. And fall some of us did, too. Well, almost. Every year, no matter how much attention was given to the positioning of the chairs on the bleachers, the exuberance reached such heights that one or two children practically fell off. Such was the price of passion soaring. I'm just glad it never happened to me.

I worked hard at Oak Knoll School, as hard as I could. Succeeding in some areas came easily for me, as I had a very high IQ, according to Mom. In the end, however, my success depended on simple hard work, which intensified with each passing year. By the time I was ten, I studied night after night with only one goal in sight: the Prize for Highest Average.

This was the most coveted award given annually at our school, Neck and neck competition did not scare me. It only made me more stubbornly determined. I simply had to win Highest Average. And I did, almost every year that I was at Oak Knoll School. But the year that counted most was 8th grade, as the student who won Highest Average in 8th grade won a full, four-year scholarship to Oak Knoll High School.

"The Prize for Highest Average is awarded to…Patricia Kentz."

When the words were called out to an auditorium filled with parents, grandparents, nuns and teachers, I knew that I had done it. Surely all the praise that people would give me would help me believe in myself. After the ceremony, my mother, brothers, sister and all of our close family friends came up to hug and congratulate me. However, when I ran to see my father, he did not hug me. He did not even seem to congratulate me. He just stated firmly, "Good job, Patsy."

Dad's words were not enough. At this point, I needed so much more from him. But he just could not give me what I needed, and I am not sure I could have received it even if he had. Even before Prize Day ended, I had already steeled myself for the next round of challenge and achievement.

CHAPTER THREE

Several times per year my desperate drive to achieve was interrupted by some of the happiest occasions of my life. These were our glorious family trips to New York City, orchestrated by my father. The days began with getting dressed up in my prettiest dress, putting bows in my hair, and weather permitting, wearing my winter wool coat with its fur collar and matching muff. Then the hour-long journey to New York began, and culminated in the grand turn down a huge hill into the dark recesses of the Lincoln Tunnel.

I busied myself in the tunnel by counting every emergency phone that whizzed by, waiting for the moment when light returned and I could finally feel the abundant aliveness of New York City.

I am sure my love of The City was something Dad passed on to me. He loved bringing us into New York and making the day special. These days were always special, whether they included Broadway shows like The Sound of Music or Man of La Mancha, tea at the Palm Court of the Plaza Hotel, or my personal favorite, an after-dinner trip to Rumplemayer's, home of the most delicious mint chocolate chip ice cream in the world!

There was only one problem with these gala events. On almost every occasion, we were nearly kicked out of the restaurant. Not because we were rude or did not pay the bill. It was simply because we stayed so late laughing and talking that we were asked to leave so the restaurant could close.

In addition to our New York visits were the annual trips to Atlantic City, long before it became laden with casinos. Hotels so large they took up entire street blocks, overlooking the Boardwalk, where every year the new Miss America was rolled in on a stupendous float.

Atlantic City meant going to the Marlborough-Blenheim Hotel with Dad's extended family. This included Grandfather Pop-Pop, Great Aunt Josephine, Great Aunt Elizabeth, Great Aunt Agnes (who was a nun), and Great Uncle Ambrose. These great-relations were very important to Dad growing up since he was an only child. Years later, the love of all of these men and women then flowed to us, my father's children.

Every night we each dressed in our finest clothes to have dinner together, but before we sat down at the very large table, we walked through "Peacock Alley." I don't know how it got this name. There were certainly no peacocks in the alley. And it was not painted in peacock hues. I guess it must have been because everyone who walked through the alley was expected to strut like a peacock.

Peacock Alley was the connecting bridge between the older Marlborough part of the hotel and the newer Blenheim part of the hotel. The bridge was lined with glass walls from floor to ceiling and on each side of the alley were chairs, where hotel guests sat and relaxed before dinner.

As we Kentz children were generally the only people in the hotel under fifty, we were accorded quite a bit of attention by the Peacock alley guests and I, for one, loved it! When I walked through the alley and heard the subtle oohs and aaahs as the elderly women commented on my dress, bows and shiny patent leather shoes, I felt like a princess. A few times I invented the excuse of searching for my "lost Pop-Pop" so that I could strut through the alley again to look for him.

At dinner, we were on the American Plan, which meant we had course after course of food, starting with shrimp cocktail and finishing with homemade ice cream.

While in Atlantic City, we never ate lunch - just a big breakfast and a big dinner.

Grandfather Pop-Pop would look at his four grandchildren with delight as we each told him about our day. As always, there was no shortage of conversation.

Everyone at the table had something to say, and again, the Kentz Klan was the last to leave the dining room. At this late hour, though, Peacock Alley required no pomp and circumstance. We ran through the Alley gaily, filled with the excitement that in seven short hours, another day at our beloved Atlantic City would begin.

I loved it all but the best part of Atlantic City by far was the time we spent at the beach. All of us loved the ocean, including my parents, who spent considerable time at the beach when they were growing up. Together we stood brave in the face of the waves that threatened to crash down on us. Some of us chose to "duck and submerge", while others chose to leap and emerge, beyond them.

As the wave came rolling toward us, Dad would exclaim, "Everyone, get into position!"

At first we did not know what he meant. After all, how can one stand in position as one is about to be rolled and tumbled by the force of a huge wave? It did not take long to figure out what Dad wanted. He loved his four charges to always be positioned in this order: Girl, Boy, Girl, Boy. So we quickly tried to get into Girl, Boy, Girl, Boy position, only to be laughing hysterically as the wave dismantled the order in a matter of seconds. At night, one of us reminded Dad of his ridiculous request and he laughed at himself uproariously!

CHAPTER FOUR

As the summers came to an end, I knew my determination to succeed would show itself perhaps even more strongly than the year before. Now on my walks home from school, I no longer gazed at the beautiful Summit homes. I spent this time reviewing what I needed to do in order to perform well at school the next day. Or I imagined myself being a star on the hockey field or the basketball court, depending on the season. Everything, at this point, was focused on achievement.

On one autumn day, however, at the start of the new school year, my planning was interrupted as I heard someone cry out, "Minky, Minky." Has anyone seen Minky?"

I stopped to watch the new family who had moved into 1 Surrey Road, about an eight-minute walk from my house. The mother was standing in the yard, calling for Minky. There were two boys playing touch football in the front yard, seemingly oblivious to the missing Minky. A few minutes later, their father joined in the game. Then I noticed a young girl in a pink sundress with big pink ribbons in her hair, who also seemed indifferent to the missing Minky, preferring her Barbie doll instead. Then another girl ran into view. She seemed about my age and wore a sailor's hat on top of a long ponytail that trailed down her back. The sailor's hat went flying in a second as she fell on the grass with a large Golden Retriever who was doing his best to kiss her profusely. "Sandy, will you cut it out" she protested over and over while laughing hysterically.

At this point, the missing cat, Minky, dashed madly across the yard. The football game came to an abrupt end, Barbie was left on her own and everyone, including the young girl and her golden retriever, ran to welcome their black cat back home.

I sat and watched all this from the other side of the street and wanted to be part of it. I knew exactly what it was like to have this much fun with my brothers and sister, but at our home, things were different. We did not feel as free. I wanted to experience this freedom.

It did not take long for the girl with the sailor's hat and I to become inseparable. Her name was Marianne Angermueller and, miraculously, she and I ended up in the same class at Oak Knoll School. We walked to and from school together each day, sat next to each other in the classroom, played together after school and then did our homework together in the evening. We were both very good students, though never competitive. When I was with Marianne, life seemed more like an adventure than a challenge. She was never short of creative ideas and I loved helping her bring them to life.

Our large backyard with its wooded area at the far end seemed a perfect place for a clubhouse. I took old chairs from our dark and damp basement, found wooden boxes for tables and placed candles on top of them, for a touch of elegance. The sign at the entrance carried a bold statement: "M and P Clubhouse - Members only." This was distressing to my brother, Andrew and Marianne's brother, Victor, who wanted to join the club. However, as co-presidents, Marianne and I were in charge and stood our ground.

Andrew and Victor could come into the clubhouse only if they paid dues and did daily jobs, such as running into the house and bringing back whatever cookies and candy they could find for Marianne and me.

Our clubhouse, though, came to an abrupt closure. Dad came home one day and became quite upset that we were using chairs from the basement. It did not matter to him that they were old and musty, he was just upset to see them used. At times, he found it very difficult to handle any change in our daily routines.

I began spending more and more time at the Angermueller's because I felt so happy there. It was chaotic at times, but it never seemed tense. Often Marianne's father sat at the kitchen table, an island of calm in the middle of the goings on around him, and sketched his five children and told fascinating tales about them. One day, he sketched me into the family photo and told a fantastic tale about me also. I loved that he included me in his sketches and I began to sit next to Mr. Angermueller whenever I could, waiting to see the sketches and hear what tales he had to tell about me! Secretly I wished Dad could be more like Mr. Angermueller. Most of all, I loved staying at their house for dinner. Granted we might have just had a bowl of cereal and an English muffin, but it did not matter.

Dinner at our house was different, more like a state function than a family gathering. We ate in the formal dining room, with a chandelier that hung large above our heads. Each globe of the chandelier glistened over the formalities of the room: the large mahogany table with its crisp white linen tablecloth, the thick gold brocade curtains which were closed as we sat down, the mahogany chest upon which Mom's shiny silver service rested, and the candles which were lit hurriedly by one of the children. Sometimes when I entered the room and took my seat, I felt like a princess.

I sat with Maryanne on one side and Mom on the other. I did not move from that seat for my whole life. Dad loved order – everyone in their place - and I noticed that I liked order too.

I made a habit of looking into the large, gold-embossed mirror that hung on the wall opposite my seat. Inevitably someone would find me staring at myself in the mirror. Everyone thought it was vanity, and maybe it was, but I think those long stares in the mirror were really a way to prove that I existed and had worth. If I could not feel it within myself, then I allowed the mirror to prove it to me.

But when I left the mirror's image and came back to real life, I generally noticed that the four of us were having a lot of fun together. As always, the feeling of having Maryanne, Rick and Andrew around me lifted me. It did not matter that I was lost in the midst of them. They were my camouflage. I felt safe and happy in their presence.

It was not unusual to have guests at our dining room table. Both my parents knew how to be good friends and they encouraged us to be the same. One night we had a special guest, my guest, Marianne Angermueller. I knew our dinners were very different than her family dinners, but I hoped she would have a good time anyway. She did, that is until the very end of the meal.

It was our family's custom to say the Catholic Rosary at the end of dinner. To save time, we did it while we were washing the dishes and getting ready for dessert. The whole scenario looked a bit preposterous, but we became accustomed to it and did not think twice about it. So it never occurred to me to prepare Marianne for the prayerful end to our meal.

Dad would lean back in his armchair, take his glasses off and then bellow, "Hail Mary, full of grace, the Lord is with thee.

Blessed art though among women and Blessed is the fruit of thy womb, Jesus."

At this point, the four of us would yell out over the din in the kitchen,

"Holy Mary, Mother of God
Pray for us sinners
Now and at the hour of our death
Amen."

I can't say it was a particularly prayerful response, but we managed to yell it loudly enough so that Dad could begin the next round of Hail Marys. This was our nightly custom. I didn't tell Marianne about this custom, though even if I had, I thought that surely she would be with us in the kitchen. But she wasn't. Dad insisted that Marianne's guest status pre-empted her from doing the dishes. She replied saying that she loved doing dishes, but he was adamant. Guests were to stay at the table and relax with him.

So with bowed head and hands clasped in prayer, Marianne sat as Dad bellowed Our Fathers and Hail Mary after Hail Mary for fifteen minutes. She heard the muffled laughter in the kitchen and wished to God that she could be part of it, but instead she adopted the most pious demeanor she was capable of and held on until the final Hail Mary was yelled out to the kitchen.

When it was over, her pious look vanished quickly. She looked me straight in the eye and told me that she would never come to dinner again if she had to say the Rosary at the table with my father. And she never had to…Mom and I made sure of it.

My friendship with Marianne softened my life. She clearly did not feel the desperation to achieve that I did. So when I was with Marianne, I relaxed, at least somewhat. However, when I sat at my desk I was determined to master anything on the page in front of me. It did not matter if I was interested in the subject matter or not. My preferences played no part in this process. I was defiantly determined to prove to my father and everyone else that I was smart in school and successful.

Apart from the respite of time with Marianne, I lived with this determination from September to June, when summer vacation began. And then, the best time of all began: our month long vacation at Hampton Beach, New Hampshire.

CHAPTER FIVE

Every year in mid-June, the family piled into the station to begin the 8- hour drive to Hampton Beach, New Hampshire. It was here that we enjoyed a month at Mom's childhood beach home.

When we turned the corner onto "J" Street, I could the see the waves from the car window and started to relax. The month at the beach was a hiatus from self-imposed demands, and the fear that was their origin. Most of all, it was a chance to feel special.

A multitude of aunts, uncles and cousins gathered at the beach house, in addition to my grandmother. Dad did not stay with us during these gatherings. He drove back home, and drove back again to pick us up at the end of our stay.

There were a total of twenty-five grandchildren all together; Nine from New York, twelve from Massachusetts and the four of us from New Jersey. It was not possible for all twenty-five grandchildren to come at the same time to visit my grandmother, but the twelve from Massachusetts and the four of us did come together every year.

The sixteen grandchildren and six adults squeezed into two houses on the property. The large, green wooden house was called "Rita", named after Mom. The smaller, darker-colored house was called "B and J", named after Mom's two brothers. Since the adults had rooms to themselves, this meant that the multitude of cousins slept in beds together. Except for me.

I don't remember ever being singled out in my childhood for anything, mostly because I did not ask to be singled out for anything. In Hampton Beach, though, I was singled out and to this day, I don't know why.

Grandma had her own tiny room, whose window opened directly to the ocean breeze, filling the room with a rich smell of salty air. Her bed was a double size, though creased down the middle with age. The mattress, at this point, was really only suited for one person, but every night it held two, Grandma and me.

When I got into bed each night, I often wondered why I was the one grandchild chosen over all the others to sleep with Grandma. Whatever the reason, I know that when I entered my side of the bed and rolled into the crease next to her, I felt a wonderful peace.

Every morning, Grandma and I woke early before anyone else and tip-toed together down to the front porch. There we sat in matching rocking chairs, rocking and talking, until the rest of the sixteen children wandered in. My heart widened with Grandma beyond my fear and ruthlessness and I will never forget this gift she gave me.

When everyone was awake, Grandma began the job of cooking breakfast for all of us and she seemed completely energized doing it. Afterwards, we all headed to the beach. We walked single file on the narrow sidewalk. One child, then another, then another, all wearing flip-flops and dragging large, multi-colored beach towels.

We ran into the sea, made sandcastles and played ball for hours. When we weren't playing, we slept. We slept on the beach for hours at a time, soaking up the warmth of the sun while generally mindless of its burning rays.

Those were happy days, and the nights were wild with fun. Every night, all of us, except for the babies, headed to the casino. Not a gambling casino, but a casino filled with games and surprises for children of all ages.

I could try to grab a furry stuffed animal in a glass cage with a pair of big scissors for 5 cents or I could play Skeeball rolling the balls furiously up the alley in search of the holes for 10 cents. I could go into the House of Horrors and scream just for the thrill of screaming at the horrors I had seen countless times. Or I could spend my money on the many treats, including Cracker Jack and Cotton Candy. Each decision was important, as my money had to last the whole month. Despite how frugal I had to be, I always walked back to Grandma's house filled to the brim with the fun of the night, as well as a Milky Way in my pocket just for her.

When my father arrived to pick us up a month later, it was hard to believe the month was already over. On the last day, my mother dressed the four of us in our best outfits for the annual home movie. Every year, my father stood in front of us, movie camera in hand, and filmed us walking hand in hand with Grandma down the street. The footage never varied from year to year. It did not have to because the feelings of joy and happiness were always the same.

With each new September, school started again. I seemed to start each year with an equal combination of excitement and great determination. But by the time I started high school, there was less excitement and more determination. By then, things had changed. With earning the full scholarship to Oak Knoll High School came the expectation that I would do very well. My sister, Maryanne, had left home to go to college. But, most of all, my beloved friend, Marianne, was not going with me to Oak Knoll High School. She was going to the public school. Bereft of my Maryanne Kentz and Marianne Angermueller, and carrying the pressure to prove that I deserved the scholarship, I began to lose myself in achievement in a way that I had never done before.

CHAPTER SIX

When I told my mother about the blood I was coughing up, she seemed alarmed. I supposed I should have been too, but at this point, I did not register too much pain in my body. I was able to carry on, despite any pain that came my way. So I often lived with bad headaches, but never told anyone about them. The blood, however, I could not ignore.

I remember being happy to see Dr. Clarke. He lived down the street from us, very close to the Angermuellers. He seemed so friendly, always waving to me on the way home from school.

At the first visit, he just said that he needed to order some x-rays. On the second visit, he had the results. At 15, I had a bleeding ulcer, a condition usually reserved for highly stressed executives. I did not really understand what it was, but remembered that two years previously, my father was hospitalized for a bleeding ulcer. Now, in yet another way, I was just like my father.

When Dr. Clarke told me I had an ulcer and explained what this meant, he asked about pressures in my life. He asked if I thought I was pushing myself too hard, and asked if I was trying to gain someone's approval. At this point, he mentioned my father.

I did not know how to answer him. I had long ago locked in my defensive pattern of refusing to feel my own pain. All I knew is that I *must* do very well at everything I did.

The conversation did not go any further than that. Dr. Clarke sensed my inability to converse about these topics, and my mother seemed unsure about how to proceed. Then, he discussed the many changes needed in my diet. I remember these were the same changes my father had to make a few years before.

Baby food, baby food and more baby food, I ate mashed bananas, pears, apples. Anything that could be mashed, I ate it. And milk. I drank so much milk I thought I would moo.

Slowly but surely my ulcer healed, just as my father's had. I wish I could have discussed everything with Dr. Clarke. If I had done so, perhaps I would not have needed relief as much as I did, and would not have clung so desperately to that relief when I finally experienced it.

I first tasted relief with my friend, Susan. We planned the night for weeks so that we could keep it perfectly clandestine. And we did.

My parents were going out for the evening. Susan came over for dinner and to spend the night. The part my parents did not know about was the liquor cabinet raid.

Susan and I had it all planned. We put a line on each bottle at the level it was when we started drinking, and refilled them to that level with water before the evening ended.

When the fun began, we took large Ronald McDonald plastic cups and poured a little from each bottle into them: a little gin, crème de menthe, scotch, brandy, cognac, Schnappes, bourbon, Irish Baileys' and on and on. We thought it would be more fun to combine everything into one drink!

We drank slowly, not quite sure if the taste was something we would like. Before long, we began to laugh and sing gaily, accompanying Neil Diamond in "Sweet Caroline", which was playing loudly on the record player.

I was euphoric! Free of self-doubt, free of the need to prove anything to anybody. I felt giddy with this freedom, and I did not want this feeling to end...ever.

When the clock struck twelve, we knew we needed to pack up quickly. We refilled the bottles with water, shook them up in the hope that they would not disclose their high water content and closed the liquor cabinet door tightly.

Both our heads hit the pillow with a thud. In a few hours, though, Susan was shaking me, telling me she was going to get sick - immediately. I had to think fast. It would not have been good to wake my parents, particularly my father, under these circumstances. The only option was the window. I opened it and helped Susan put her head out in the freezing cold. When she stopped vomiting, she collapsed again in a deep sleep.

In the morning, my mother woke us cheerily with the news that she made pancakes for breakfast. She said we needed to hurry, as this was the day we were going to sing at the Old People's Home, also known as Ivy Haven, in Newark, New Jersey.

My mother believed in helping those who were less fortunate, and ordinarily I agreed with her, but that day was simply not the day for singing at the Old People's Home. Of course, we had no choice. We pushed the pancakes around with our fork and collapsed into the back seat of the car as my mother made the forty-minute drive.

My mother seemed even cheerier than usual when she asked us to tell her about the nice time that we had the night before. Without hesitation, I told her we watched a great movie, while trusting that she did not hear the slight tremor in my voice.

Finally, the bouncing of the car and our delicate stomachs subsided as my mother turned into the Ivy Haven driveway. Even on our best days, Ivy Haven had always tested us. It was, after all, a nursing home for people who had no money. But today the combined smell of cleaning chemicals, urine and hospital food seemed just too much.

Our only option was to throw ourselves into song, so that's what we did. Joy to the World, Hark the Herald Angels Sing, and more. We sang every carol with all our might. Then we wandered from the hallway into individual patient rooms, keeping the same pitch going as we sang. We sang to one elderly woman after another, enjoying the thanks and smiles we received. However, one woman seemed remarkably unresponsive, perhaps in a deep sleep. So we spontaneously began to sing even louder, trying hard to impart some Christmas cheer. We stopped abruptly, however, when we heard a cry from the neighboring bed, "Don't bother singing to Rosie. She's dead."

Susan and I left the room as quickly as we could, went into the hall, looked at each other stunned and then burst out laughing!

When Susan and I had another quiet moment alone, we compared symptoms. Susan told me emphatically that she never wanted to touch alcohol again. I looked at her trying to hide my disbelief as I sensed she expected me to agree with her. Truthfully, though, I could not wait to have my next drink.

CHAPTER SEVEN

The next opportunity to taste this wonderful euphoria came on a spring night in my junior year. It was the night of a mixer at Oak Knoll. Mixers were considered a nice way for Catholic teenage girls to meet Catholic teenage boys. Oak Knoll invited the boys' school and all we had to do was show up and cruise around the room. I had my driver's license before my other friends did, so I was able to drive my friends everywhere, including to the mixer.

My parents were going to be out that evening. With their blessing, I invited six of my friends over that so that we could get dressed together, go to the mixer and then come back to our house to sleep.

My mother smiled as she said goodbye to us, watching us try on dresses and put on make-up. Once my parents' car turned out of the driveway, the festivities began with our raiding my father's liquor cabinet. We each poured a glass of whatever looked good, and I started to feel that this was going to be great night!

We made a nearly invisible line on each of the bottles before we started pouring and then when the 'raid' ended, we filled the bottles with water right up to the line. This was a great plan. My father would never miss a drop. I was having so much fun! The pressure to achieve seemed to dissolve and the feeling of being lost and insignificant seemed to vanish. All I knew is that I felt wonderful and I did not want it to end.

We all piled into my mother's station wagon and quickly chewed as many mints as we could during the ten-minute drive to Oak Knoll. I was the first one in and went right up to Mother Jean Marie, the school principal, and gave her a huge hug. Never in a million years would I have given our school principal a big hug, without the help of alcohol. Then at the mixer, I flirted with every boy I could find and danced wildly to every song. We managed to get home before my parents and made sure the kitchen looked clean. I was convinced that I had pulled it off and slept soundly, as did all my friends.

Then, on Sunday evening, everything started to unravel. I knew it the moment I heard my father say, "Hello Mother Jean Marie, how are you this evening?" I am sure she had not called to have a friendly chat with my father on Sunday night at 8 o'clock! It seemed like an eternity before my father spoke again and the words were not reassuring. "I am very disappointed to hear this. I will talk to Patsy and get to the bottom of it."

It did not take long at all before my father called out forcefully, "PATSY!"

He got right to the point. "Were you drinking Friday night?" I quickly replied, "NO!" I had not lied often in my life, yet this lie came out so fast, so easily; I surprised myself. Dad said he would call Mother Jean Marie back and explain that there must have been some mistake. As soon as the phone was free, I called Susan, whispered what had happened and instructed her to call the others to make sure everyone stuck to the same story.

That night I lay in bed, still stunned by how fast I had lied and how quickly I covered everything up. But I could not be too concerned. The prospect of enduring Mother Jean Marie's and my parents' anger was more than I could bear. I fell asleep trying to convince myself that once again I had "pulled it off."

On Monday morning, however, the Jean Marie Witch Trial began. One by one, Mother Jean Marie called each girl into her office separately and interrogated her. In between the interrogations, we whispered to each other in the hallway to make sure we were telling the same stories so we could remain united in our defense. Everyone needed to tell the same story. Everyone needed to not cave in and blurt out the truth.

At the end of the week, a week in which I could not concentrate on anything other than the Jean Marie Witch Trial, I was called into the office one more time. Mother Jean Marie stared at me, and despite her thick glasses, I could see she meant business. Once again, she asked me if I had been drinking on Friday night. This time, I broke down and told the truth. I have no idea what happened after that, no idea of what she said, what punishment was meted out or what happened to the other girls. I have no recollection of anything. All I knew was the agony of worrying night and day was over. I also knew I had to find a way to drink again, and if I needed to lie to do it, I would. I was 17, one of the brightest students in the class, popular, attractive to boys and yet none of this mattered. I wanted a drink.

The only memory I had in the aftermath of the Witch Trial occurred when my parents had a dinner party about a month later. I was in the kitchen preparing the meal for all their friends when I overheard a conversation between my father and one of his close friends.

"Fred, do you call this a drink?"

"Well, sure, Dick, what's wrong with it?"

"Well, it's water… just look at it."

With my stomach and throat very tight, I eagerly awaited my father's next words.

"I don't understand how this liquor bottle got so diluted. It must be the cleaning lady."

I breathed a sigh of relief, happy that it was just a close call.

CHAPTER EIGHT

It was time to apply to colleges and Georgetown University was at the top of the list. It was my father's alma mater. He was proud of Georgetown, had wonderful memories of his time there and was still very active in the Alumni Association. Rick was already at Georgetown and I remembered how proud he was that Rick was accepted. I wanted to go there too so that my father would be as proud of me as he was of Rick.

I had all the prerequisites to attend Georgetown. I was valedictorian of my class. I was the president of the Athletic Association, sports editor of the school newspaper and involved in many other extracurricular activities.

The wait to hear from Georgetown seemed endless. Finally, I received the news. I would be joining the freshman class of Georgetown in the fall of 1972. I did it! I was accepted at Georgetown! I could not wait to tell my father.

When I ran to greet him with the news, his reply was matter of fact. "Good Job, Patsy", had become his classic response to my achievements. His words were deflating, however, it was his tone that always secretly undid me. Curt, even stern, it demonstrated his real fear of connecting with me, though in the moments of hearing it, this interpretation eluded me.

My father's fear of connecting with me became more intense when he dropped me off at Georgetown a few months later. My mother hugged me, said how much she would miss me and encouraged me to call home whenever I wanted. My father, however, looked tense when he shook my hand and said, "Best of luck, Patsy."

But I did not dwell on my father's response. "On my own at last" was all that went through my mind when I walked into my dorm room on the Georgetown campus! I quickly entered the Pre-Med program and declared a double major in Biology and Psychology. I was on my way to fulfilling my life-long dream to become a doctor.

On the first day of the Pre-Med Chemistry class, our professor announced that we should take a long, hard look at the person on the left of us and then the person on the right. He explained that one of these two people would NOT pass the course. He spoke even more imperiously when he announced his goal: to make sure that only 50% of our group was able to continue in the Georgetown University Pre-Med program. My response was much the same as it had always been: I would do whatever it took to succeed. My defiant jaw was set. I would NOT be the student that failed.

I was always capable of great concentration. I could sit for hours and stay very focused. I had been doing this since I was a little girl and thus was all set to do it at Georgetown. I did not waste any time finding my cubicle on the fourth floor of the Georgetown University Library. It would be my home from 7 p.m. till midnight, five nights per week, for the next four years.

Despite the rigorous schedule, I was lucky to make two good friends quickly, Alice Marie and Mona. Nearly every night during the first month at Georgetown, Alice Marie and Mona came to the library around 8, found me lost in chemistry formulas and tried to entreat me to go to the pub for a beer. And every night I declined with the same words, "I'm sorry. I wish I could, but I have to study." After four weeks of the same scenario, they stopped coming to my cubicle. They knew I was driven. But only I knew that I was counting the days until Friday night when I could let go of all the self-imposed rigor and have a drink. After all, I had earned it.

From the time I arrived at Georgetown, I always had dates. The best part about going out on a date was the drinking I did with my friends before. By the time my date arrived, I was already "quite happy." Before long, it was well known that Patsy drank a lot on weekends.

Though I was much more inclined to hard work rather than introspection, I did often wonder how Alice Marie and Mona did it. They studied, did well and had a couple of drinks on weekends. They did not need to drink the way I did. Why did I have to turn into a different person every Friday night? What was so painful about my life that I had to try to forget it all every weekend? I did not get too far with these questions. As soon as I sensed any of my own pain - any fear, sorrow or anger whatsoever, I thought about something else. I did not want to feel any internal struggles. These questions were important, but it was more important that I ignore them.

A vicious circle had begun. I demanded perfection in my work so that others would be proud of me. Yet I never allowed myself to feel the desperate longing that was propelling me. Alcohol kept me away from all this pain and, in the process of ignoring it, I became even more driven. The semester ended and I not only passed Chemistry, I got an "A." The professor was true to his word; many students failed and could not continue in Pre-Med. But I would continue. For me, it was proof that my system of hard work during the week followed by the reward of alcohol on the weekend was working perfectly.

Alice Marie and Mona were now my close friends, lots of boys wanted to go out with me, but by far the most important connection I had at Georgetown was with my brother. Rick was a junior at Georgetown, captain of the basketball team and was also very handsome. All my life I sensed his protective presence around me, but at Georgetown I did not just sense it, I saw it in action every single day.

Every night, despite whether it was hot, cold, raining or snowing, Rick came to my dorm to say goodnight. He never came into the building, instead he threw a small rock at my dorm room window. When the rock hit, I jumped to open the window, ready for the late night conversation, but most of all for the first words, "Pats, are you ok?"

I always said yes, focusing less on the reply than on the wonderful feeling of being loved and protected. "Well, I talked to Mom today and she's getting over her cold. It's been snowing in New Jersey and Andrew did not have to go to school today." He talked as if we were sitting down over a cup of coffee instead of yelling from the ground to me four stories above.

He also did not seem to notice that the more he stopped by, the more the other windows began to open when the loud greeting began. The word was out and the coeds responded to the subtle message relayed through the dorm: If you open your window, you can catch a glimpse of the handsome captain of the basketball team every night around 10:30 or 11. "Call me if you need anything." These were always Rick's last words to me and they touched me as much as his first.

By the end of my Freshman year, not only was I still standing in the Chem Lab, I also had outstanding grades in every other subject. I was at the top of the pre-med class. I thought I was doing great! Others, however, did not think so.

In my sophomore year, I rented an apartment near Georgetown with Alice Marie and Mona. I was happy to be with my two close friends, enjoying the freedom of our own apartment. I continued my pattern of hard work and hard play until one night when Alice Marie and Mona asked me to sit with them to talk about something.

They looked so serious. Mona began. She explained that they were worried about me, or more precisely, they were worried about my drinking. They were concerned that I might be developing a "problem" with alcohol. I was indignant, but remained cool. After years of hiding what I really felt, it did not occur to me to do otherwise. Plus, I did not want to offend them. I hated people being upset with me!

I reassured myself that I was not an alcoholic. I did not touch a drop of alcohol during the week. Didn't even think about it. Well, perhaps this was not true. But even if I wanted some alcohol on Tuesday, I was able to control this impulse and wait until Friday. What more proof did they – or I - need? I did not have a problem with alcohol.

My mind moved quickly through this cascade of thoughts, but I revealed none of them to my friends. To Alice Maria and Mona, I simply offered my thanks for their concern and said that I would "try and cut back." I had no intention of cutting back.

What I did instead was develop a strategy. I made sure that my friends did not see me drinking at home before dates. I hid the alcohol and drank in my room. This worked. Alice Marie and Mona remained convinced that I was "trying" while I did not have to change a thing. The subject was not mentioned again that year. And, as our sophomore year drew to a close, they obviously felt that my trying was working and we happily made plans to live together for our Junior year.

CHAPTER NINE

In January of our junior year, on a crisp, cold but unseasonably sunny afternoon, Alice Marie and Mona asked if I would like to go ice-skating with them. As usual, I declined, but they were ready for it with a second round of encouragement combined with gentle pressure. The combination worked. I got my scarf, mittens, hat, money and was out the door in a flash.

At the public rink, I rented skates and charged onto the rink, though I hardly knew how to skate. Within minutes, I saw a handsome man whipping around on his skates. He seemed confident and adorable and I wanted to meet him. As he skated in my direction, I made a point of falling, as gracefully as possible, right in front of him.

After he helped me to my feet and the introductions were complete, we talked for about ten minutes, though I did not remember what was said. What I remember were his deep brown eyes, wonderful smile and the delightful sense of mischief.

When it was time to leave, he asked for my phone number and I said it loudly over the din of the Zamboni ice-cleaner twice, to make sure he heard it. Then every night for the next seven, I left the library early, hoping to find a message waiting for me. Finally, it lay waiting on the hallway table. Twenty minutes later, I had a date with John Motley.

It did not take long before John and I were seeing each other every weekend. We had fun together and laughed a lot. He had a great love of life. He also had some delightfully funny habits, including his love of vacuuming!

A few months after we met, John invited me to Boston to "meet the family." I was thrilled. My mother and I went shopping together and decided on a blue suit that made my blue eyes shine. John's parents were as welcoming and gracious as their son, and I felt at home immediately.

I offered to help John's mother prepare dinner and she asked me to go outside to pick a large bowl of peas from the garden. Of course, I was keen to make a good impression, so I was determined to bring in more peas than we could all possibly eat.

The garden was large and filled with every conceivable fruit and vegetable, including bright orange carrots and dark green beans, all lovingly tended by John's mother. I spied the peas, filled the bowl to the brim and smiled as I handed it to John's mother, asking, "Will this be enough?"

I could not quite understand her expression. It was a combination of horror and amazement. Then she burst out laughing and explained that I had just picked her entire crop of unripe blueberries!

In spite of the blueberry incident, John's mother and father could not have been more welcoming. I came away from my weekend as much in love with them as I was with their son.

In my last year at Georgetown, I was on track. I was at the top of the Pre-Med Program and destined for admission to medical school. I had dreamed of this and believed I could do it. What I could not have anticipated, though, is that I would change my mind.

It wasn't that I no longer wanted to be doctor. It was that something had gotten in the way: John. I had fallen in love with John and wanted to spend as much time as I could with him, preferably the rest of my life.

I began to agonize. I did not want to give up John. I did not want to give up my dream. But to fulfil this dream, I would be working almost round the clock for ten years. What kind of life would it mean for John and me? Would we ever have children?

I needed help and sought it from the Dean of the College of Arts and Sciences. Fr. Royden Davis was a soft-spoken and calm man, who seemed perfectly suited to his role as Dean. He was also a friend of my father's and knew my family well. When I arrived for my appointment, he hugged me and asked, "How's my #1 pre-med student doing today?"

I did not know if he would think the same of me by the end of the conversation, but I had no choice but to tell him that I was not sure I wanted to go through with it. Fr. Davis listened patiently to all my concerns and then asked simply, "Have you ever thought of Dental School?"

Why would I ever want to put my hands in someone's mouth for the rest of my life? I did not say it out loud, but that is exactly what I thought. Before I had a chance to raise even one of my many objections, Fr. Davis asked if I would like to visit the Georgetown Dental School and meet with one of the dentists who taught there. I agreed and within a few minutes was sitting opposite a woman dentist named Dr. Martin.

I noticed quickly that Dr. Martin was attractive. She wore a stunning blue print dress with a starched white lab coat on top. I liked the dark blue embroidery that announced to the world that she was indeed a Doctor.

She welcomed me into her office and listened to my concerns. Before she had a chance to reply, there was a knock on the door. A young dental student politely asked, "Dr. Martin, I am ready to begin the periodontal graft. Could you come now to check the preparation for the surgery?"

I watched the student and Dr. Martin closely. In a year's time, I could be this student and in a few years time, I could be Dr. Martin. And I could do all of this without sacrificing my life with John. Dentistry was not looking so bad after all, especially when I reminded myself that I had always wanted work with my hands and become a surgeon.

Dr. Martin and I spoke for over an hour. She explained how the lifestyle of a dentist was very different than that of a doctor. She also explained how the training was very different, too. By the time I walked out of Dr. Martin's office, I had made up my mind. I walked back to Fr. Davis' office and resolutely announced, "I am going to be a dentist."

I felt more than relieved. I felt elated and quickly called my parents to share the news. My mother told me she was thrilled with my decision. My father responded differently. In his forceful voice, he asked if I realized what a big decision this was and then expressed concern that I would regret my choice. I tried to explain my decision, but my defense was weak. I felt crushed. I wanted to <u>hear</u> that my father was proud of me, and even more, I wanted to <u>feel</u> that I was proud of myself. Both of these senses eluded me at the time.

CHAPTER TEN

In the fall of 1976, I started Georgetown University Dental School and moved in with John. We rented a small townhouse in Washington, DC. We could not afford a lot of furniture, but that did not matter to us. We were so happy to be together.

In the evenings, I made dinner while John set up the card table in the living room. He always lit candles to give the basic furnishings a touch of romance. After dinner, I studied while John prepared for his sales calls the next day.

On the weekends, the card table remained closed as we treated ourselves to dinner at some of Washington's many beautiful restaurants. I loved to get dressed up each weekend and walk arm in arm with John around the city.

John was very good to me and he was also very proud of me. Whenever we ran into people we knew, he couldn't wait to tell them that I was in dental school and that in a few years, I would be a practicing dentist. I smiled as he and others focused on me with pride. But, sadly, this smile was just superficial. I spent a large part of my life denying how much I wanted to be loved and approved of, while holding on tightly to a rigid lifestyle that might guarantee both. Now, at last, when love and approval were offered so freely, I simply was incapable of taking them in.

So I continued in the pattern that had worked so well. Hold on to the rigid schedule of hard work all week, and let loose with alcohol on the weekend. Despite how much this pattern looked like it worked, it didn't.

In the first two years of dental school, the dental students studied with the medical students every morning. In the afternoons, the medical students went to the hospital while we went to the Dental Lab and practiced "drill and fill" on mannequins.

During the second two years, we rotated through two-month tours of each speciality in dentistry, including periodontics, orthodontics, crown and bridge and others. I was one of six female dentists in a class of 150 dental students, but in my speciality rotation group of thirty students, I was the only female.

On the first day of my Prosthodontic tour, the chairman of the Department, Dr. Todd, came to greet us. He seemed to be looking quite closely at me in the front row. After he offered his introductory remarks, it became clear why.

"I do not believe that women should be dentists", he said while staring at me.

"This is a male profession."

Within seconds, he could not contain his anger at all. Glaring at me, the only woman in the room, he said, "Dr. Kentz, I am going to make the next two months so difficult for you that you will wish you'd never chosen dentistry."

My mouth dropped open, but I was determined not to cry. No one had prepared me for this attitude, but I knew what to do. After all, I'd had a lot of practice. I held my jaw strong in defiance while silently asserting "I'll show him."

And I did.

I finished all the requirements for the tour two weeks ahead of schedule. What should have taken eight weeks to complete took me six. This was unheard of, I was told.

This did not satisfy Dr. Todd. He was on a mission to prove women were not suitable for dentistry and I was to be his proof. As I prepared to relax for two weeks while the other students finished, Dr. Todd called me into his office. He was clearly furious that I had finished ahead of the others.

"I want you to sit right here while I call each one of the patients you worked on during this tour. If any one of them – *any* one of them – is not completely happy with your work, then you will have to redo the work. Do you understand?"

I nodded, but realized that I could not really feel much fear of him. My defiance had served me well. All I wanted to do was get back at him, one way or another.

But as I sat and watched him call each of my patients, I allowed myself to wonder what I had done that was so bad, and why he found me so despicable. I recognized the pain of these questions instantly – this deep self-doubt, the deep sense of unworthiness – but I did not linger on them at all.

Dr. Todd called each one of my twelve patients. Each reported that s/he was satisfied with my dental work and some even sang my praises. This seemed to make Dr. Todd even more upset. "Dr. Kentz, you are dismissed" was all he could say. I left the office, resisting the urge to slam the door.

Overall my life in dental school was very similar to my life as an undergraduate. I studied hard all week and rewarded myself on the weekend. It seemed to be working as well as before. I was definitely one of the top dental students, had many dental school friends and the professors, apart from the infamous Dr. Todd, seemed to like and respect me. From my vantage point, there was no problem and I assumed others felt the same. One day, though, I happened to glance at the Dental School Student Newspaper, specifically at the gossip column on the back page. The column contained tidbits of gossip about students, who were identified simply by their initials.

"P.K. – Sloshed"

Instantly my mind raced to the inevitable question. Was P.K. me? But I knew the answer even before I scanned the list of students who might have similar initials.

The next month, the gossip was more pointed:

"P.K. – Sloshed again."

The following month, the gossip became more of a plea:

"P.K. – Sloshed again. Does she have a problem?"

I felt sick each time I read the gossip column and wondered if I did have a problem. No, I quickly dismissed the thought. Once again, I reassured myself that someone who did not touch a drop of alcohol from Sunday night to Friday night, week in and week out, could not have a problem. However, the gossip column did teach me something. I needed to hide my drinking better.

So I hid my drinking better, continued to do well at school and fell more and more in love with John over the remaining years of Dental School. The four years came to an end quickly and in a dramatic way.

About a week before graduation, the Dean of the Dental School called me into his office. I had never been in his office and had no idea why he wanted to see me. He was an illustrious figure. I could tell this by all the framed degrees on his wall. But I did not have time to stare too much at the degrees or the plush office as he got straight to the point.

"Dr. Kentz, I wanted to let you know that you will be receiving the highest award at Graduation next week. I called you in today to congratulate you personally."

I left the office in a daze.

ME?

I felt like a ballerina catapulting to the sky!

I ran home to John, who was bursting with joy as he showered me with hugs and kisses.

I called my sister, who repeated over and over how proud she was of me.

I called my mother, who started to cry through her words of praise.

But when I spoke to my father, he repeated the three words he said every time I achieved anything in life. The same three words in the same tense tone:

"Good job, Patsy."

Why my father's words affected me the most, despite the overwhelming praise and delight of others, I did not understand. But they did, and not in a way that helped me heal. Instead of allowing myself to feel the pain of fear, sorrow and anger, so I could finally begin to release it, I just felt crushed, defeated, hopeless and defiant. As always, I knew I could find relief with a drink.

After graduation, I started work as an associate dentist in a large, well-established dental practice. Yet there was another, more significant change in my life. For the first time in many years, I did not have to study at night. I had no time to develop other interests during my years of academic rigor. Now as a result, I had no idea what to do with myself.

It seemed only natural to start to have a few cocktails in the evening. It did not take long for this to become a routine. I worked hard and did well during the day, then came home and made a drink while preparing dinner for John and me. By the time John came home, I was already "feeling good" and talked enthusiastically about my day.

John was not a big drinker. In fact, he hardly drank at all. He did not seem to mind the "let loose with alcohol" weekend pattern of the previous few years. I guess he thought I deserved it, given how hard I worked during the week. Now, however, my drinking was excessive and it began to take a toll on our relationship. At first, it was the little incidents at home. I cut myself with a sharp knife and needed stitches. I fell down the stairs a few times and had large bruises. Then the incidents began occurring outside our home. I drank too much and embarrassed him in front of his friends, many of whom were his business associates.

He discussed this with me on a regular basis and I was always full of remorse. I never wanted to hurt John or embarrass him. Not then, not ever, but I was caught in a cycle that I was powerless over and I did not even realize it.

After our discussions I continued to drink, but worked very hard to make sure it did not take a toll on John or on our relationship. However, after a few months or even a few weeks, there would be another incident, followed by another discussion, followed by more remorse and more promises to change.

Gradually, more and more of my friends were getting married. This added to my ache inside that John and I were not married. Whenever I spoke to John about it, he replied in the same way, "I am not ready to be married yet."

This went on for several years, but I sensed that his reluctance had more to do with my drinking rather than his ambivalence about marriage. I also sensed that our relationship was going to end if I did not do something about my drinking. So I went through a period of white-knuckling it. Through sheer will power, I controlled my drinking. This was not easy at all, but I continued to remind myself of what the consequences would be if my drinking became out of control.

I was able to maintain this for months and my relationship with John improved dramatically. Still, it came as a complete surprise when John proposed to me over the Christmas holidays of 1984. When we announced the news to our families, there was tremendous celebration. Finally, Patsy and John were getting married!

John gave me the most beautiful three-carat diamond engagement ring. I stared at it in disbelief. It was the most beautiful ring I had ever seen, and it was on my finger! I had never felt such happiness. I adored John, and now we were going to spend the rest of our lives together. We planned to celebrate the good news with his family on Christmas day.

John's grandmother was the matriarch of an aristocratic Boston family. The Motley family, with all the aunts, uncles and cousins, spent Christmas day at their grandmother's enormous apartment in an exclusive neighborhood of Boston. Christmas dinner was catered and served by several maids; a butler answered the door and the dress code was black tie.

It was important to me that I spend Christmas morning with my own family in New Jersey. So I planned to fly to Boston in the afternoon, then go directly to John's grandmother's home for the celebration. I was beside myself with excitement but believed a few drinks would help me stay relaxed, while also make me a little more interesting and exciting. So I fixed a couple of vodka and sodas to drink on the plane.

When I got off the plane, I ran to John and stumbled into his arms. He looked at me with utter desolation.

"My God, Patsy, have you been drinking?"

The only way an alcoholic knows how to respond when confronted about their drinking is to lie. So I lied. I told John that I was dizzy and weak from the turbulence on the plane. When we arrived at his grandmother's, John explained to everyone that I was not feeling well. I spent the rest of Christmas day sleeping it off in his grandmother's guest room.

John was shaken. I could feel it. I quickly tried to rescue the situation with a promise that I would stop drinking completely. What I did not realize was that I could not stop drinking. For the next six months, I was very careful to sneak my drinking and felt I was successful. John seemed subdued compared to the pre-wedding excitement I was feeling, but I attributed this to all the many details we had to keep track of.

The wedding was orchestrated by my father, with my complete blessing. No one could plan and organize events like my father. He was an amazing organizer, possessed a true sense of style and beauty and enlisted the help of others easily.

My father spared no expense for me. The wedding party alone was lavish: ten bridesmaids and ten groomsmen! More than two hundred guests would make their way to my hometown church, and then proceed to one of New Jersey's most beautiful country clubs. There we would enjoy a 5-course, sit down dinner and a night resplendent with music, champagne and toasts. I could not wait for my wedding day! I also could not wait for my honeymoon. John had planned a trip of a lifetime: three weeks in Europe at 5-star hotels in every city along the way!

I had just one more week to wait and the fairy tale wedding would begin. I was singing with joy as I packed my suitcase, ready to go home to spend this week with my mother and Maryanne. I could not understand why John seemed even more subdued when he came into the bedroom.

John sat down on the bed next to me and took my hands into his. His eyes were moist with tears as he looked directly into mine. He said he had been anguishing for months over his decision.

"What decision?"

My mind raced everywhere, but landed at the inevitable before John even spoke the words.

"I just can't go through with this marriage."

I did not speak. I just shook, uncontrollably, for many minutes. John held me. I could feel his love, but did not stop shaking. Finally, when the tears and shaking lessened, John explained.

He did not pretend there was any reason other than my drinking. But he did not punish me for it, either. John sat in front of me, heartbroken, and I sat in front of him, heartbroken.

Of course, I pleaded, promising anything that would change John's mind. It was futile, though, and I knew it. John would not marry someone with a drinking problem who refused to accept it.

The fairy tale wedding was cancelled, the luxurious gifts returned and the 5-star hotel rooms went empty. I still packed my suitcase, but this time it was to leave the home and man I loved.

CHAPTER ELEVEN

I don't remember those next few weeks of my life. Friends said that my new townhouse was very nice, but I did not pay any attention to it. I simply thought of John constantly. I wanted to call him, but knew I couldn't. Once in a while, he called to see how I was, but when I heard his voice, I could not bear the pain. He must have sensed this because he stopped calling.

I continued to work every day, solidly for nine hours with only a short break. I stayed focused and committed to providing quality dental care to my patients. However, when I came home, all of the emotion held back through the focus of the day soon overwhelmed me. I reached for the vodka bottle trusting that it would bring me relief.

I continued this pattern of hard work and solitary drinking for months, until I knew I had to start getting out and seeing people. Calling my friends and crying about what had happened was wearing thin, for them and for me.

So I began to attend medical and dental professional meetings, where I knew I could regain some sense of self-worth and perhaps even meet someone. The months of solitary drinking had warped my thinking: I was determined to prove that if John "did not want me", then I would find someone who did.

It did not take long.

Dressed up and looking good, I always had a few drinks before arriving at the meetings so that I seemed bubbly and happy. I met many dentists, doctors and surgeons and it did not take long for the phone to start ringing. I began going out almost every night of the week with different people, but the person who most caught my eye was a surgeon named Greg.

For our first date, Greg took me to an exclusive Washington restaurant. It was one that John and I had always wanted to go to, but never felt we could afford. I spent hours getting ready and had a few drinks to help the evening go smoothly. All my advance planning worked. Greg seemed to like me and asked me out again on the next day.

After a few weeks of seeing each other often, Greg invited me to his home, a luxurious mansion outside of Washington. I had to catch my breath when we drove down the long, winding driveway. The view was breathtaking. Standing gracefully next to the swimming pool were many full, manicured boxwoods with pink and white blossomed trees hanging overhead.

There was a four-car garage that housed a shiny black Mercedes convertible, a Jeep for weekends and some other cars for purposes I could not even imagine. Nothing, though, could have prepared me for the house itself. It was a palace.

Greg held my arm as we walked up the grand staircase to the second floor, but I could not resist reaching out to touch the thick, shiny wood banister. I wondered if the trim was real gold, while trying to make sure I did not seem in awe of it all. I could not hide my surprise, though, about the many bedrooms. Why did one man need five bedrooms, each with its own fireplace and each larger than the next?

Greg muttered something about his parents visiting and then mentioned his young daughter from a previous marriage. I did not pay much attention to his words because I was already beginning to imagine myself living in this wondrous home.

The surprises kept coming as we made our way back down the emerald green, carpeted staircase, past the large framed photographs of his ancestors. The living room had a grand piano that would have been the envy of any concert pianist. The dining room had an antique table that seated sixteen people easily, and twenty in a squeeze. The kitchen had every conceivable modern appliance a chef could hope for. But what struck me the most were the flowers. They were everywhere, large vases of all kinds of flowers, everywhere. I did not have the nerve to ask Greg if they were automatically delivered weekly, but I suspected they were.

I sat at the kitchen table, with its six handsome wooden chairs, watched the fire glowing in front of me and felt that this house could be a perfect place to live. Greg interrupted my daydreaming when he came in with the dinner that he had prepared on the large deck attached to the kitchen. Greg opened an expensive bottle of wine, but I was careful, very careful. I did not want to ruin anything.

When Greg brought me home that night, I could not sleep. I poured several drinks while I sat and thought about the evening. Yes, Greg was handsome, but certainly nothing like John. His personality was not exciting like John's, but he was not completely boring either. After my third drink, I reasoned that no one would ever be like John and that I just had to get used to this fact. With more slurred thinking, I talked myself into believing that I could grow to care for Greg, no matter how little chemistry there was between us. And, of course, there was the house. The house would make up for so much, I told myself, as the vodka eased me into a deep sleep on the couch.

Greg and I continued to see each other every week and, before long, I was spending every weekend at the palace. However, on one occasion, Greg invited me to spend the weekend with him at the Homestead, a celebrated and very expensive resort.

When we entered the women's boutique on the resort property, I expected to only window shop. But Greg insisted I try on several outfits, all of which I had to admit, looked good. Greg could not contain himself. He purchased many expensive outfits for me, so many that we could hardly carry the garment bags and boxes up to our room.

I kept trying to manage all of this from my mind instead of my heart. From this abstracted place, I came to the conclusion that I could not turn my back on Greg and what he was offering. After all, I was over thirty years old and did not want to be alone forever. A successful man was enthralled with me and wanted to spend his life with me. It seemed only logical that I would want the same. So when Greg placed an enormous diamond ring on my finger a month later, I said yes.

My friends and family worried that I was rushing into it. After all, it had only been six months since the wedding with John was called off. I insisted otherwise and my stubborn insistence prevailed.

Once again, my father took on the job of planning the wedding. Again he spared no expense, planning an exquisite celebration. Since Greg had been married before in the Catholic Church and was divorced, we could not be married in a Catholic Church. My father arranged for his friend, a judge, to perform the ceremony at another exquisite New Jersey country club.

When the sun came up I was excited, almost too excited. I looked at my cream colored wedding dress with its expensive lace and its extra long train and could not believe that I was going to be a bride. All eyes would be on me. I would be a beautiful bride, at last.

It seemed only natural to pour a vodka and coke and sip on it while I was getting dressed. It also did not seem out of the ordinary to make several bottles full of vodka and coke for the reception, though I did sense I should hide them.

My father's plans were perfect; everything flowed. Although he simply could not have planned for one thing, that the bride would be drunk even before the wedding cake was cut.

My mother spotted that I was about to fall over on the dance floor and told Maryanne to get me off it and downstairs as fast as she could. I don't know how Maryanne did it as I could barely walk, but she did. Without too many words, she and my mother managed to get me dressed in my going away outfit, a blue seersucker suit that my mother and I bought on a much happier day, weeks before the wedding.

The photographer managed to get one shot of me waving goodbye at the car. I smiled happily, not having any sense of the damage that had been done to so many. That night Greg would barely talk to me. The next day Greg's parents seemed in shock. But most of all, I remember the devastation on my mother's face. I especially remember her eyes, those light blue eyes, crushed in sorrow.

I could not bear it. I could not bear any of it: the sorrow, the shame, the guilt, the fear of reprisal. It was too much and I did not have any idea how to change it. I was caught in the nightmare of alcoholism and the consequences were only just beginning.

Before Greg and I married, I knew that he and his ex-wife, Susan, were in court negotiating the custody of their daughter. They had been divorced two years and there was animosity between them. Susan was a well-known physician in the Washington area and, given that she and Greg were both successful professionals caught in a custody battle, the media began to cover the case.

When I married Greg, I had no idea how all-consuming the custody battle would become. It was on our honeymoon in Florida that I had my first sense of what our lives would be like. Greg spent most of his time on the phone with his lawyer, and I spent most of my time listening to Greg tell me about the phone calls.

I had married a man I did not love, but, at the same time, felt the compassion anyone feels for a father who wanted to see his child. I wanted to support Greg as much as I could, and I did not dare cause any more scenes like our wedding reception. For these reasons, I told Greg that I wanted to stop drinking and knew I needed help in order to do it.

A few weeks later, I attended my first AA meeting and decided to stop drinking, one day at a time. Initially, Greg was thrilled yet he also had another response to my sobriety. He seemed uncomfortable, even threatened, by my strength and self-confidence that increased as each alcohol-free day passed.

In addition, the demands and uncertainties of the legal battle were taking a huge toll, emotionally, physically and financially. Greg was frustrated and angry. He could not show this in court nor display this to his patients if he wanted to maintain a viable medical practice. The only place he could vent this pent-up rage was at home with me.

At first, it was verbal. He told me he did not want me to go to "those meetings." It was brainwashing, he asserted, and he did not like what I had become. Then his complaints became edicts: he ordered me to stop attending AA meetings completely. Despite the orders, I kept going to AA every night after work. When I arrived home at 8:30 p.m., I trusted he would be too tired to fight about it.

Greg's stress mounted by the day. The custody battle was fiery, with each side making allegations of all kinds of abuse of the little girl who was caught in the middle. Both Greg and his former wife were prominent Washington, DC professionals, in a contested custody battle. The media simply could not get enough of the story!

Every day, morning and night, there were reporters parked outside our house, trying to get a glimpse of Greg. They eventually resorted to hydraulic lift boxes, sneaking them a bird's eye peak into our bedroom.

Eventually, they won. I suppose I should have expected it because God knows they were determined. It was on an uneventful Saturday afternoon that I went into town to do errands when I saw Greg's face staring back at me from the cover of Time Magazine. Not just a small photo in the corner, but the entire cover given over to Greg and the custody battle.

I did not rush to open the magazine because I was too scared of what I might find. I just prayed that I would not find myself inside the pages. But there I was, pictured behind Greg walking into the courtroom, in a full four-page article with many photos.

My response was instinctive: I needed to protect myself professionally. I was a recovering alcoholic and this was not something I wanted the world to know.

I contacted a lawyer. I posed my one and only question: What would it take to keep my history of alcoholism out of the press?

$30,000, was his reply.

Payable up front, with the guarantee that there would be no mention of my drinking in any publication.

I refused to look shocked, despite the fact that the figure was a chunk of my annual income.

I paid it. I didn't really have a choice. When reporters climb into elevator-like boxes at any hour, day or night, to get a picture of me in bed with my husband, they would certainly have no qualms with telling the world I was an alcoholic in recovery.

I was careful to ensure my patients did not know of my involvement in the case. When I married Greg, I kept my family name and so remained Dr. Kentz to all my patients. Also, when I accompanied Greg to the courthouse, I held a black coat over my face. If I did not, the entire population of the Washington DC metropolitan area would see me on the news that night.

I thought I was doing a good job. I was not drinking. My patients did not make a connection between the heated custody battle and me, so life at work was steady and tranquil. And my lawyer fulfilled his guarantee: there was no mention of my drinking in any publication or news broadcast.

It was in this relative calm that the physical abuse began. I should have expected it, but I didn't. I thought if I kept my world alcohol free and calm, it would simply stay that way. The physical abuse began one night over dinner, one that I made especially for Greg, as it was his favorite. He had not even touched it, though, when he yelled, "Do you call this dinner?"

Rage flowed through his arms as Greg picked up the plate and threw the dinner in my face.

I screamed.

Greg responded by also throwing his glass of iced tea in my face and stormed out of the room.

I grabbed a towel and ran outside. On the steps, I sobbed, wondering if this nightmare was real. I knew I was not imaging it, but I also did not understand how this could be happening to me. I did not understand it at all. I desperately wanted to drink but knew that drinking would only make things worse. A few months of sobriety had taught me this.

I cleaned up the kitchen and went upstairs to get ready for bed. When I got out of the shower, Greg was standing there handing me a towel. He apologized repeatedly, saying that he never meant to hurt me. Over and over again he told me much he loved me. Then, with a maniacal smile on his face he said, "Why don't you come to bed and I will show you how much I love you." I was soon to know what the words "battered wife" really meant.

The rage began to escalate and, for reasons that remained elusive at the time, I put up with it. This all changed one day when it became obvious that the consequences could become life threatening.

There was nothing dramatic about the morning. No yelling, no upsetting phone calls, and Greg and I had become accustomed to the media right outside our door. There was really no way to explain why Greg turned to me and yelled, "You are a zero. A worthless piece of shit. It makes me sick to look at you."

With that, Greg picked up the kitchen chair and threw it against the wall. I lurched in the opposite direction and tripped over a heavy wrought iron antique, which crashed down on my right wrist. The pain was overwhelming for a few seconds, then my wrist began to throb intensely. In the moment, I had no choice but to ignore it.

I grabbed my purse and ran as fast as I could. I have no memory of driving to work, but I do remember the gasps of the office staff when they saw my mascara-streaked face and hugely swollen wrist. I mumbled something about tripping over an antique, not caring whether they believed me or not. I was in shock, heart-broken, furious and disbelieving that I had allowed my life to come to this.

The fury, however, won out and propelled me. I drove to my doctor's office and he confirmed, through x-rays, that my wrist was badly damaged and that I could not work for six weeks. From there, I went straight to an AA meeting. By this time, my AA friends knew what was happening at home so I did not resort to a half-truth as I had at the office. I told it straight and they listened.

I was advised to develop an exit plan, a way to get myself and my belongings out of the house. At first, I thought this was extreme, presuming again that my identity and worth depended on proving just how tough I was. But I could not ignore the pounding pain in my wrist, which seemed to coincide with a pounding thought in my head: I DESERVE BETTER!

My wrist healed in six weeks and during this time, there was relative calm at home. Greg was subdued and kept to himself. Despite that, my AA group was not convinced these episodes of abuse had passed. At one meeting, a woman named June, my closest friend in the group, handed me the key to her house. She made me promise that I would come there anytime, day or night, if I needed to get out of my own home. When she hugged me, I felt the force of her love and the warmth of security.

It was not long before I needed the key to June's house. One week after I accepted it, Greg directed his most intense rage at me. I should have seen it coming. It had been a bad day in court and it took him three times as long to get home from the courthouse after a massive snowstorm. It was late in the evening. I was undressed and ready for bed when Greg started yelling. Instinctively, I ran toward the bathroom, hoping to lock myself in. I was not fast enough. Greg pinned me against the wall, his eyes crazed with rage.

"You are a zero.

You are a sorry excuse for a person.

And I cannot stand to look at you even one more minute."

I heard this before, and before, I partially believed it. But this night was different. I remembered June's embrace, remembered that I put the extra car key under the mat as my AA friends advised, and most of all, I remembered the fledgling belief that I deserve better. I ran out of the house, just as he released me from the wall and reached for a lamp.

It did not matter that I was running in a light nightgown in 20-degree weather through 12 inches of snow. I was running for my life and I knew it. I locked the doors quickly and started the car, ignoring that Greg had draped himself across the front of car, banging on the windshield furiously and yelling uncontrollably.

I turned the wheels of the car, hoping that sanity would prevail for a few seconds and that Greg would get off the car. He did and in that instant, I slammed on the accelerator and roared away down the icy driveway. Greg jumped into his car attempting to follow me, but my head start made the difference. When I turned onto the main road, he was not in sight. I arrived at June's at 10:30 p.m., shaking and in tears.

June stayed by my side for hours. She held me tightly until I stopped shaking. She prepared a warm bath and helped me climb into it. She put extra blankets on my bed and waited until I fell asleep. We did not talk about what happened.

When I woke, June was sitting in the rocking chair next to me. Her smile and the slow cadence of the rocking chair lulled me beyond the terror of the night before. We talked about what happened and she, like many of my AA friends, spoke earnestly about the necessity of getting out. I certainly did not rule out leaving Greg, but later that morning I drove back home.

Over the next couple of months, I needed to escape two more times to June's house. Each time the scenes were worse. Finally, I moved beyond my refusal to face what was completely obvious to everyone else. I had to get out of Greg's house, and I had to get out fast!

I talked to my friends in AA about my decision and could see that a lot of them wanted to say, "It took you long enough", but were kind enough not to. Considering Greg's rage, I knew my exit needed to be planned perfectly. Everything that was mine needed to be removed from the house, without Greg knowing about it. A friend of mine offered her garage and I accepted, bringing a box or two at a time without Greg noticing any changes. Thankfully, Greg was calmer during this time.

Finally on October 2, 1987, 14 months after we were married, I was leaving Greg. I left for work that morning as if it were a normal day, yet all my appointments had been cancelled. The office staff had strict instructions to tell Greg that I was with a patient and could not be disturbed, no matter what time of day he might call.

Greg always left for work a half-hour later than I. Then, he would drive by the shopping center to get on the highway. I waited in the parking lot of the shopping center with two AA friends, Dave and Alan, who both had trucks. At 8:03 that morning, Greg drove by. At 8:04, Dave, Alan and I drove back to the house. These two kind men followed me from room to room as I pointed to beds, dressers, tables and chairs. While they loaded my furniture, I loaded the clothes. We moved fast and in silence, propelled by the anxiety of Greg's making a surprise appearance. In less than two hours, the trucks were packed and we were on our way to my new apartment, rented only a week before. Dave and Alan unpacked my furniture and helped to bring the apartment to life. I had my own home and I was safe, yet all

I wanted to do was cry. Tears of joy and sorrow co-mingled and poured freely down my face.

When the phone rang, I jumped. No one had this number except the receptionist at work. Tentatively I picked up the phone and heard her quivering voice. Greg had been calling constantly. When he could not reach me, he showed up at the office. She was terrified by his yelling and banging on the desk. As she was picking up the phone to call the police, he stormed out as fast as he stormed in.

My God, if he is this angry now, what will happen when he arrives home and finds everything gone, including me, was the only thought I had. I was terrified but kept repeating over and over to myself that it was impossible for Greg to find me. Only the receptionist had my number and she had sworn not to give it to anyone. And only Dave and Alan knew my address.

I leaned back in my chair, looked at the new clock on the wall and realized that Greg would now be reading the note I left him. I kept it simple:

"Greg,
The marriage is over
Do not try to contact me.
Patsy"

No matter what his response, the fact was that I was safe. And I was determined to keep it this way. Of course, it did not mean that Greg did not try to reach me. He called the office constantly and was rejected each time. Finally, I realized that the receptionist could not defend me forever. On the next day, I agreed to speak to Greg.

It was predictable. He pleaded that I come home, promising to change. I had heard it all before and this time I did not fall for it. Finally, he cried out, alluding to what I sensed was his deepest motive, "Don't you realize what this will do to my custody battle?"

I knew what it would do and I did not care.

The pleading turned into abuse. I listened to Greg's rant that I was a worthless person for less than fifteen seconds. I still was not sure how much worth I had, but I knew I wasn't worthless. I hung up on Greg and never spoke to him again.

CHAPTER TWELVE

My apartment was not grand like Greg's estate, but it was mine. With my love of interior design inherited from my father, I filled my new apartment with bright colors, happy designs, hardy plants and throughout the process, brought myself back to life. My life was simple and happy. I loved work, loved my apartment and grew to realize that AA was a true salvation. I went to meetings weekly and stayed sober.

After about five months, though, I began to drink again. I don't know why. All I know is that I was lulled into thinking I was fine, and that a drink or two would not hurt. I also know that deep down I was looking for a high, something that would be more exciting than my simple life.

I kept drinking but kept going to AA. I figured that as long as I was handling the alcohol reasonably well, there was no real problem. Then, I started to skip meetings, just one or two. Friends from AA called and I could hear the concern in their voice. I reassured them, skipped more meetings and eventually they stopped calling.

I worked hard during the day and got drunk every night. This went on for several months. Finally, I was drinking as heavily as I was when John cancelled the wedding two years before. When drunk, I picked up the phone and called my family and friends. I slurred my speech and kept repeating myself. I sensed that everyone wanted to get off the phone, but short of hanging up on me, they did not know how to do it.

My family was getting frustrated with me. My drinking had been a problem for over ten years and while I'd had some periods of sobriety, they were by no means a sure thing. Their frustration reached a peak on a cold day in Massachusetts. My mother's only remaining brother, whom she adored, had just died. Virtually all of my cousins made their way to New England for the funeral. When I arrived, I staggered up the aisle of the church. When my mother turned from her front row pew and saw me weaving up the aisle, she looked horrified. Within seconds, her horror turned to desolation. After the funeral, my brother, Rick, took me back to the hotel to sleep it off. He had only one thing to say, "Don't you dare leave this room", and only one question to ask, "How could you do this to Mom?" I heard his words, but was too lost in my own alcoholic world to make sense of them.

Of course a rift was developing between my mother and me. She could not bear to watch me destroy my life. She had seen it before, as one of her brothers was an alcoholic and she could not bear to watch it happen again, this time to her own daughter.

Nonetheless, she invited me to come to New Jersey to spend the weekend with her two sisters. She knew I would love to have a weekend with them, playing bridge, shopping at the outlet malls, watching a movie together until late at night. I was the designated cook that weekend, and happy to prepare a meal they would love. I poured a drink while cooking dinner and so slurred my words when I announced, "Dinner's ready." When I carried the chicken casserole to the table, I tripped, sending the casserole flying across the floor and onto the walls.

My mother could not look at me. My aunts put me to bed. I slept until my mother walked into my room at 8 am the next morning and announced, "Pack your bags. I want you out of here in an hour. I cannot have you here because I will not watch you kill yourself."

I was gone in an hour. On the ride home, it did not occur to me to stop drinking. I felt I just needed to control it better. Yet, I also felt I needed AA again.

This dichotomy, wanting to drink in a controlled manner and at the same time wanting to be part of AA, had characterized my life for years. I refused to accept, deeply accept, that I was powerless over alcohol and that I could not drink without hurting myself and others. I refused to accept that I would never heal unless I was willing to feel emotional pain. I also refused to accept that seeking my Higher Power, something that had been nurtured in me from an early age, was pivotal to my sobriety. Despite my ambivalence, I returned to AA and was greeted with loving support and a clear message:

"We will love you until you love yourself."

I wish I could say this beautiful message changed my life. However, I was lost in the distorted perception and disordered thinking of alcoholism. I decided that I just needed a partner.

Since I did not want to go to bars to meet men, I decided to tell my friends that I wanted to meet people. I had a couple of blind dates, but nothing particularly exciting followed. About six months later, my dental hygienist told me about someone whom she thought I might like to meet.

A few days later, I got a call from Jim Ondo. We talked for about forty-five minutes on the phone; he sounded wonderful. He asked me to have dinner with him on the following Saturday.

A few hours before he arrived, I began trying on many different outfits to see what looked best. I decided on a pink flowered sundress, white sandals and pink clips in my hair to match the pink in my dress. When the doorbell rang, I wanted to make sure I did not look as excited as I felt. It was hard to hide my delight, however, when I opened the door and saw a very handsome man. He smiled and said, "Hi, I'm Jim."

We went to a beautiful French restaurant, where we sat for two hours without a lull in the conversation. Afterwards at my house, he kissed me goodnight and asked if he could see me again. I was thrilled, smiled and said, "I'd love it!"

When I closed the door and sat down in the living room, I reflected upon the evening. Jim was so handsome. He was six feet tall, had a strong, kind face and beautiful blue eyes. When he smiled, his entire face lit up. He graduated from West Point, just completed twenty years in the Army and planned to retire within the next year. He had two children from a previous marriage, who lived in California with his former wife.

The following weekend we went on our second date to Great Falls, Virginia, where we had a delicious picnic lunch that Jim prepared himself. We watched the kayakers gliding down the river, laid in the sun and enjoyed all the delicacies he had prepared. I was amazed at how comfortable I was with him already. Around 5, we packed up to go home, but neither of us wanted the day to end. So we rented a movie, sat on the couch eating popcorn and just enjoyed being together.

We continued to see each other every week and before long, I was falling in love. I told Jim that I had a "problem with alcohol." His reaction was much better than I anticipated. He seemed pleased to hear that I was on a path to recovery. Once again, though, I was not telling the whole truth. Although I did not drink when I was with Jim, I was still drinking.

A month later, I received a surprise phone call from my brother, Rick, who said he was coming to Washington and wanted to have breakfast with me. I was delighted, especially since this meant that I could tell him all about Jim. We agreed to meet at his hotel around 9 am. I went to Rick's hotel feeling relaxed and looking forward to our visit. When I arrived, Rick hugged me and suggested we go up to his room for coffee.

When he opened the door to his room, I walked in and gasped. There in front of me were twelve people, all of whom deeply cared about me. My parents, brothers, close personal friends and wonderful office staff were all seated in a semi-circle around the room with their eyes on me.

A man that I had never seen came forward, introduced himself as Dr. Simpson and explained that he was the Chairman of the Caring Dentists Committee. I looked at him with confusion and disbelief. The Caring Dentists Committee?! What was the Caring Dentists Committee anyway? And, most of all, why did they care about so much about me?

Dr. Simpson then spoke, "Your family and friends are here today because they love you. They are also very worried about your drinking. Each person has something to say to you."

My father spoke first.

"Patsy, I just cannot stand by and watch you destroy your life."

There was no anger in his voice, just sorrow and tears flowing liberally down his face. I had never seen my father cry before this moment.

My mother followed, "Sweetheart, you know how much I love you. I would give my life for you. I have been watching you kill yourself for years. The pain I feel watching this is beyond anything I have ever known. I cannot stand by and watch this go on and on. I am begging you to get the help you need."

I heard them, but I was not listening. I sat absolutely frozen, not allowing any of their words or feelings to touch me. When feeling began to register again in my body, there was only rage. How dare all these people gang up on me! They had no right.

Each person had his or her chance to speak. I remained immune to all of their pleas, preferring to stay outraged at their performance, which appeared to have been planned for weeks.

After all twelve people spoke, Dr. Simpson announced, "We have arranged for you to go to a treatment center in Williamsburg. They have a bed available for you today. Do you have any questions?"

All twelve people stared at me with much the same look in their face - a heartfelt plea that I would agree to go into treatment. I did not need long to reply to their plea,

"Thank you all very much for your concern, but I don't need to go the treatment center. I will just go back to AA. I can stop drinking on my own."

Ever defiant, ever refusing to yield to the truth of my life, I ignored their plea.

"If you take this option, Patsy, you will lose your dental license," Dr. Simpson said firmly.

"Well you really don't give me any choice, do you?" I replied immediately.

"You do have a choice. You can do it your way, but if you do, you will no longer have a dental license."

I agreed to go to the treatment center.

The intervention came to a quick end. People hugged me as they walked out the room saying how proud they were of my decision. My face was stone cold. I felt furious and betrayed. When my mother hugged me and said that she would be praying for me, I did not reply. I did not even look at her. I walked away from her in silence.

Dr. Simpson and his wife followed me in their car back to my house. They were going to wait while I packed my suitcase and then drive me to Williamsburg. When we walked in the house, Dr. Simpson commented on the beautiful home I had. I ignored his comment. I walked upstairs to pack my suitcase and Mrs. Simpson followed. Though I was quick to reassure her that I did not need her help, she explained that she had to be present while I packed. I quickly figured out why. If she had not been there, I would have run to the closet and finished the entire vodka bottle before leaving home.

The ride down was certainly not pleasant for the Simpsons. They both tried to make small talk while I maintained a severe scowl and answered in monosyllables. After awhile, they gave up and we just drove in silence.

When we arrived, I was brought into the detox room, where a nurse came to do an intake interview. She asked how much I drank per day and I told her that I had one or two drinks in the evening. Fortunately, she knew that I was lying, as most people in detox do.

Dr. Simpson waited to say goodbye. His parting words were heartfelt:

"I have done a lot of interventions, but this was one was remarkable. Your family and friends love you very much. Please don't forget this."

I glared at him, uttered a perfunctory thank you and discovered how cold I could be.

I was escorted into my bedroom by a woman named Anne, who explained to me that she was my counselor. She explained that her assistant Mary would now go through my belongings. My defiant jaw throbbed with rage.

Mary went through every single item in my suitcase to make sure that I brought no alcohol into the center. She opened containers, smelled things, shook things until everything was checked thoroughly.

Having passed the test, I was invited to get a good night's sleep. Was she crazy? I lay on my bed and stared at the ceiling the entire night. It was a nightmare from which there was no escape; there was not a drop of vodka in sight.

I was allowed one phone call and, of course, I called Jim. When I told him that I was at a treatment center in

Williamsburg, he was just as shocked as I had been. He then told how much he loved me and said that he would be right by my side through this journey.

This was a treatment center for health professionals: pharmacists, vets, nurses, doctors, dentists, all who were licensed to practice in Virginia. Everyone had their careers and everyone had their private hell of alcoholism. Everyone remembered how awful their first few days of detox were and so reached out to me with kind hearts. Once the fog and physical pain of detox lifted, I started to feel better and entered into the daily program without resistance.

We had lectures, group therapy and individual time with our counselors. There were 15 women health professionals at the center at this time and we lived in apartments within walking distance of the center. We bought our food together, ate together, cleaned the apartment together and had ample time to get to know each other. These friendships were different than those I had in school. Only another alcoholic knows the same self-loathing, shame and despair that an alcoholic feels. Embraced by others who did not judge me, I started to relax and laugh again. I had not really laughed or had fun in years.

I stayed at the center three months and as I walked out the door, I was very different than when I walked in. I gained a new understanding: I could face life alcohol free. I could feel pain without caving in. I could cry and not feel weak. I did not have to prove anything to anybody. And I just prayed that all of this change would last.

As soon as I got home, I checked the schedule of AA meetings. We all were told that if you did not get to an AA meeting on your first day home, the odds of remaining sober were slim. I knew I did not want to descend into that hell again and drove to the first AA meeting in my area.

I was so happy to be back with Jim, who remained supportive during my entire time at the center. It felt as if we were both falling in love all over again, but something was different. I was sober.

The entire time I was in the treatment center, I was in touch with the dentist with whom I had been practicing for ten years. He was happy to hear how well I was doing at the center and told me he looked forward to my return to the practice. When it was time to go back to work, I called to ask when he would like me to start. He simply said, "Patsy I am not going to renew your contract. I don't want an alcoholic dentist working in this practice."

I said, "Thank you" and hung up.

I was in shock; I never expected this at all. I was swirling in the emotions of anger, fear, sorrow and shame. That night, Jim held me in his arms and told me how much he loved me. He assured me that I would find another job in no time and said, "Don't forget, you are the best dentist in all of Virginia."

Days turned into weeks and weeks into months. I immersed myself in AA, got a sponsor and read the literature, none of which I had done with any real commitment before. And with all of this, my relationships with my family began to heal.

I was ready to work again, but had no idea where to look. I decided to call Dr. Simpson, hoping he would forgive, or at least, forget my angry coldness several months before. Though I struggled with shame, I reminded myself that he had helped many dentists, like myself, and that he did not judge any of us. Besides, I really needed a job.

Dr. Simpson could not think of anyone who might be able to help me until the last minute of our phone call. He suddenly remembered an old dental school friend of his, Dr. David Johnson, who had his own practice in Oakton, Virginia. I did not wait a minute to pick up the phone and call Dr. Johnson. When I reached him, I could hardly believe his words, "My wife and I have been praying that God would lead us to a new dentist for our practice. Why don't you come over tomorrow morning so that we can talk?"

When I woke the next morning, I felt this was the new start that I'd wanted so much. My black leather shoes were shining just as they had when I walked into Oak Knoll's kindergarten thirty years before. Although my mother was not actually with me telling me I looked pretty as a picture, I knew she was with me in spirit.

When I looked at Dr. Johnson for the first time, I relaxed completely. Everything about him was reassuring: his eyes, his face and, in particular, the way he shook my hand and waited for me to sit down first conveyed his respect for me. I could not hold on to any embarrassment in the face of this man's kindness until, of course, the moment when I had to tell him that I was an alcoholic.

"I need to let you know that I am a recovering alcoholic. "

I had practiced the words many times so that they would not be tinged by embarrassment. After all, how could this dentist believe in me if I did not believe in myself? Recovering from alcoholism is a day by day process and on this day, sitting with Dr. Johnson, I was sober and committed to recovery. That's all that counted.

"I need to let you know that I am a recovering sinner."

Dr. Johnson's words were as straightforward as mine. I tried not to look dazed by his reply, but really had no idea what he was talking about. Dr. Johnson explained that he was a born again Christian and that he ran his dental practice according to Christian principles. I had heard the expression before, "Born Again Christian", but really did not know what it meant. I found out soon enough as in his next breath, Dr. Johnson offered me a dental associate position in his practice, starting the following Monday!

Driving home, I was filled with joy! I felt that the past and its stigma were behind me. I had a new start and wanted to make the most of it. My contract at the old office allowed me to send announcements to my patients, informing them of my new location. Most of these patients had been with me for ten years, and over 95% of them followed me to this new office.

It is a big adjustment to start work in a new dental practice. The staff, patients and equipment are all new. Of course, I wanted to do a good job because I was so grateful that Dr. Johnson hired me. I did not want to let him down.

I was nervous the first week. I wanted so much to be successful at this new practice, but my success depended on so many other than myself. Most of all, this depended on the relationship with my dental assistant. If she and worked well together, then I would succeed. If we did not, then I would fail. It was as simple as that.

By the end of the first day, all of my concern vanished. My new dental assistant, Carol, was brilliant in every respect. She was brilliant with her hands, with the patients and also with me. Anyone observing us would think we had worked together for years.

That night, Carol called me at home to ask if there was anything she could do to make my transition easier. She clearly wanted me to succeed at my new job, and to this day, I wonder if she knew why this mattered so much.

Dr. Johnson's deep spirituality permeated the entire practice, from the morning prayer circle to the heartfelt good-byes we gave each other at the end of the day.

Everything about the office was "born again Christian." Having grown up Catholic, this was also an adjustment. The reception room had every Christian magazine available on display and there were bibles on every table. The music piped throughout the office was Christian songs and almost all of the patients were born again Christians!

During my first week at the office, I was scheduled to see one of Dr. Simpson's patients for a root canal. After I explained to the patient what to expect from the procedure, I asked if she had any questions. She answered, "While you are working, tell me about your faith."

This caught me off-guard. How was I going to have a one-hour monologue about my faith? I answered simply, "I have faith", and put the drill in her mouth.

Dr. Johnson's confidence in me as a dentist was exceptionally strong. When he traveled, he always selected me over the other dentists to see his patients, even though they had worked at the practice much longer than I. Even the Salvation Army patients, whom we saw in our practice at no charge, repeatedly asked if they could see "that blonde dentist."

I worked for Dr. Johnson for six years. These were some of the most easeful years of my life. I had all the patients I could hope for and their loyalty reinforced my self-confidence as a dentist.

CHAPTER THIRTEEN

During this time, Jim and I had grown very much in love. On June 22, 1991, we were married at a small ceremony in the Catholic Church in Reston, Virginia followed by a reception at our home. Jim's children, Jennifer and Jason, flew in from California for the wedding. All of my family attended the celebration as did many of my friends.

It was one of the happiest days of my life!

Shortly after we were married, Jim retired from the Army as a Lieutenant Colonel. His retirement ceremony was held at the Pentagon. Jim was so handsome in his dress army uniform with his many medals on his jacket. One of the best ways I would describe Jim is that he is a man of honor. After the ceremony, there was a lovely reception. One of the many toasts offered was by his good friend, Dave. He talked about Jim's many wonderful qualities and finished by saying, "And I am so glad you found your rocket scientist."

Afterwards I asked Jim what Dave's comment meant and he replied, "When we were first going out, I told Dave all about you. I told Dave you were not only beautiful but you were also brilliant, just like a rocket scientist." As we drove home, I leaned back and smiled.

At home, life flowed. Jim and I loved our life together in the house that my mother helped me purchase. It had been a display home years before within the planned community of Reston. Not nearly as large as the other

Reston homes, its smaller size made it seem special. Like a dollhouse in the midst of vast mansions, it radiated love in each small detail.

All the rooms were different, each with a different color scheme and décor of its own. My favorite was the Florida Room, bright with colors of yellow, coral, pink and green. It served as a vibrant reminder of all the happy times I had at the beaches of New Hampshire, New Jersey and Florida as a child. The living room, in contrast, was handsome and formal in teal blues and grays with silver framed photos scattered across dark, shiny mahogany tables.

Our home was orderly, which Jim appreciated. Years of military training had instilled an appreciation of order, and even though I am not an officer in the military, I also love order. We were well matched and together created a place of ease and enjoyment for ourselves and our two cats, Ashley and Kelly.

Jim was the love of my life and my best friend. We both worked hard at our offices every day and so looked forward to our dinners together in the evening, eager to share the news of the day. After dinner, we watched a movie or a favorite TV show. This was highlighted with a treat of cake, ice cream, popcorn, whatever sounded good.

Though I am sure our weekends together would seem mundane or even boring to most people, they were very special to Jim and me. We cherished the simple things, like going grocery shopping together! In addition to strolling down the aisles of Giant together, we stopped at the pet store where we played with the puppies and kittens, admired the beautiful birds and listened to the huge talking parrot! After the pet store, our next stop was the bread store, where we tried all the many samples and then made our bread selection for the week. Next stop, of course, was Starbucks, where I never deviated from my vanilla no-foam latte with extra cinnamon, sugar and cream! Coffees in hand, we sat on an outside bench, watched the passers-by and even made some new friends.

It might be hard to imagine why such mundane activities meant so much to me. After years of drinking, hiding it and feeling such remorse, going into a pet store, having a delicious coffee and doing grocery shopping with the man I love felt like heaven to me!

On Saturday nights, we never missed the opportunity to go out for dinner together. I loved getting dressed up just as I did when my family and I went to New York and Atlantic City so many years before. Walking arm in arm with Jim, I felt so happy, so secure and so loved.

When we returned home from the restaurant, Jim tucked me into bed, gave me a kiss and told me how much he loved me. And he has done this without fail every night of our twenty years together!

There was something else that was special in our life, which was taking care of our nephew, Peter. As Jim and I knew we would not have children, taking care of our nephew was a treat! Peter lived with my brother, Andrew, and his wife, Ellen, in a large red brick home in stunning Georgetown. It was always a joy for Jim and I to spend time with Andrew, Ellen and Peter.

Chapter Fourteen

For three years, life flowed at work and with the simple pleasures at home. Then things changed at work, first subtly and then dramatically. Dr. Johnson decided to move into pre-retirement and come into the dental office only two days per week. He chose to delegate the day to day operations of the practice to Maxine, the office manager, who rose to the challenge with a frightening zeal. While Dr. Johnson put a premium on kindness in every interaction, Maxine seemed to put the same premium on harshness. While Dr. Johnson talked engagingly, Maxine barked as if we were new recruits in the army, rather than people who had worked together for years.

Maxine's pet project was the parking lot. She was passionate about its orderliness. To ensure that it stayed orderly, she developed her parking lot fine program. If any one of us parked outside the lines of our parking space, we were given a fine. It is not that we had to hand over a quarter; our pay was actually docked a dollar with each offense. The parking lot inspector, Maxine, checked the lot after we arrived in the morning and again in the afternoon, just to ensure that there were no post-lunch encroachments. Sometimes she took one of us outside to point out that even though we had not actually touched the line, we were quite close to it or perhaps even too far from it, and so was issued a written warning.

At first, it seemed humorous, something to laugh at together. Over time, it was less so. Since Dr. Johnson was at the practice so little, he could not see what was happening or admonish Maxine for becoming a mini-dictator. Morale started to drop. People did not want to come to work, and when they were there, dreaded seeing Maxine who seem to always have many criticisms for each of us.

In the midst of all this unpleasantness, Dr. Johnson came into the practice one day beaming and asked if Jim and I could meet with him on the upcoming Saturday. While I could tell from his expression that there was nothing to fear, I still could not have guessed the reason for the meeting.

When we arrived, Dr. Johnson was again beaming. He ushered us into his office where his wife was waiting for us. A large basket of fruit was on the desk, clearly a gift for me. I had no idea what I had done to deserve this. Dr. Johnson got straight to the point:

"Patsy, as you know, I have been working on a semi-retired basis for the last year as I would like to retire in the next twelve months. I have been a dentist for thirty years and, together with you and others, have built this into a successful dental practice. I must consider carefully who to pass this practice on to and, after a lot of consideration and prayer, I feel certain that you are meant to have this practice. You have displayed such skill as a dentist and such commitment to our patients. I would like you to succeed me as the owner of this practice."

Dr. Johnson then explained that he knew it was a big decision and that he fully expected me to take my time to give him a response. He reiterated that he hoped I would accept his invitation so the practice could be a center of excellence in the community.

Now I was the one beaming! Maybe I did not have much belief in myself, but I could not deny the belief Dr. Johnson had in me. He could have chosen either of the other two associates. Actually, he could have chosen any dentist he wanted, but he chose me. The only problem was I could not buy his dental practice.

I did not have to deliberate at all nor did Jim. We simply did not want to accept the financial responsibility of a large dental practice. I especially did not welcome taking on a sinking ship and, whether Dr. Johnson knew it or not, the practice was a sinking ship, thanks to Maxine.

I was not particularly concerned about Dr. Johnson's reaction to my decision not to buy his practice. After all, there were many dentists who would jump at the opportunity to purchase a successful dental practice. Plus, he did say that he understood that it was a big decision.

When I told Dr. Johnson that I could not accept his invitation, he was visibly upset. I could see it in his eyes and feel it in his voice. Even though he said it was a big decision and that we must consider it seriously, I could tell that he wholeheartedly believed I would buy the practice and succeed him.

I could not change the look in his eyes or the flat tone in his voice. He was devastated by my decision and seemed to even be somewhat betrayed by it. Nothing changed on the surface. I went to work every day and did a good job. Yet Dr. Johnson no longer seemed particularly interested in me or my work. Something had broken between us and it was beyond me to fix it.

Months went by with little communication between us until one day when he looked particularly tense and asked me to come and see him. He asked me to sit down and then he said, "Patsy, our walk together is over."

He explained that my time at the dental practice needed to come to an end. He said he appreciated all that I had done for the practice but that he did not need me to work for him anymore.

I did not see this coming and it did not make any sense. Over time I began to feel the unfairness of it all. How could I be both the star of the practice and then be fired all within two months? I was certain there was more to it, perhaps a lot more. I suspected he wanted to hire someone who would take over the practice, but Dr. Johnson never revealed to me the reason for his sudden decision.

The thought of looking for another associate position was very discouraging; I just did not have the energy to do it. Jim, feeling my weariness, suggested that I open my own practice. This idea had never occurred to me but did sound exciting. I called Carol and asked what she thought.

"If you do it, I will be right by your side," she stated matter-of-factly.

I knew that she, like so many of us, was unhappy at Dr. Johnson's office, but it was also true that she had been at his office for sixteen years. So I had to ask, "Would you really, Carol, do you really mean you would come with me?" I cried into the phone.

Somehow I knew that if Carol and I took this on together, we would be a success. And we were.

We found the location for the new office. It was a quarter of a mile from Dr. Johnson's office, but he graciously agreed to the new location, saying, "We don't own our patients. They are free to see whatever dentist they want."

Once again, I sent out announcements to my patients and, once again, almost all of my patients followed me to the new practice.

Opening a dental practice is a major undertaking because there is so much equipment that must be purchased, either new or second-hand, and also because so many staff members need to be interviewed and hired. In addition, there were many services that needed to be put in place for the staff, including, health benefits, and retirement programs, not to mention a security system for the entire office.

Carol was right by my side when I met with the various representatives. And it was good that she was because I invariably opted for the gold-deluxe option of whatever was on offer. Thankfully, Carol intervened before I sold my life away with a polite, "Dr. Kentz, don't we have to run this by the accountant first?" Later I often asked her where I would be without her and she would always reply, "In debt.... in a lot of debt." Honestly, the truth is that I simply could not have done this without Carol.

On December 2, 1996, the dental practice, Patricia Kentz, DDS, LTD opened its doors. It was a relatively unique practice because there were no men working in it. Dentistry, traditionally a male-dominated profession, resulted in most dental practices having one or more men. Mine consisted of only females.

We allowed the feminine to shine through in all of our choices. The colors were remarkably soft; there were always fresh flowers; the lighting was warm and the music, soothing. These choices did not go unnoticed. Patients often commented how relaxed they felt upon entering our front door. It is as if they forgot they were coming to see the dentist, which is exactly what we hoped would happen!

We were busier than we could ever have anticipated, in part because so many patients followed me to my new practice. Many of these long-time patients were invited to the open house, held a few weeks after the practice opened. My mother flew down from New Jersey and joined my friends, brothers and colleagues for the celebration. My father was not able to make it and I was disappointed more than I should have been.

Lying in bed that night, I understood why self-respect eluded me year in and year out. Yes, I heard people's congratulations and their generous expressions of praise, but their accolades could not touch me deeply. It was as if I was on a stage, acting rather than being present. While on stage, I did what it took to ensure that others would praise me, knowing all the while that when the stage curtain closed, I would still be left with the feeling that I did not deserve any of what they said.

If I had to explain why I started to drink again in the midst of this great success, I would say that it was because I could no longer live life on a stage, and I did not have the resources to get off.

Jim saw the drinking start again and was perplexed. He wanted to believe the on-stage Patsy as much as I did. But the on-stage Patsy was cracking, yet again, and did not know how to help herself. All the promises to "never do it again" were empty and Jim knew this. He decided to act before it was impossible for me to even get on the stage at all.

It was a sunny Friday in June, my day off. I was in my glory lying on our deck in the sun, feeling carefree and delighted to enjoy another three-day weekend. When Jim called to tell me he was coming home early, I was so happy. When he walked in the door and suggested we go out for lunch, I was thrilled. While busily shedding bathing suit for sundress, I did not hear the doorbell ring. However, I had no trouble hearing Jim's words when he welcomed the visitor, "Hello, Dr. Simpson, Please come in."

It was, of course, another intervention. Three people sat in front of me: Jim, Dr. Simpson and Sharon, a friend from AA. Jim and Sharon spoke similarly, stating they would not stand by and do nothing as I destroyed my life. Dr. Simpson's message was more riveting: my dental practice would be closed immediately if I did not go into treatment on that day.

In some ways, there was nothing different. I was lost in the nightmare of alcoholism, and again, would not commit myself to recovery. Yet in other ways, everything was different. This time, I did not fight their words. I did not fight the way I had years before. I knew they were right and I knew that they cared. On the surface, this looked like a terrible defeat, but I knew it was the beginning of a real triumph, the triumph of love in my life.

That night Jim and I sat together. There were silences, but they were not painful. Jim loved me and wanted me to heal, no matter what it took. I needed help to recover and I was going to get it. It was that simple. The next day, I left for Tampa, Florida, where I spent a year in rehabilitation.

CHAPTER FIFTEEN

Sobering up on the plane, I collapsed into great shame and self-loathing. What was the matter with me? Why did I stubbornly refuse to face the truth of my life? And why did I insist that I live my life on a stage, pretending to the world that I was not struggling as deeply as I was? And most of all, why had I refused for almost twenty years to accept the love that so many people offered so freely? I felt that I must be a terrible person and, frankly, given all the lies, the broken promises and all the betrayal of the previous twenty years, I did not think that my perception was totally inaccurate.

As before, I quickly learned that time in rehab is not meant for wallowing. Within two hours of arriving, I was interviewed, put on a number of medications to help with the detox effects from alcohol, and met with various counselors who were assigned to me for the duration of my time in rehabilitation.

After five days in detox, I moved into a common area, where there were four houses that shared one large back yard. Approximately twenty women lived in these houses. All were health professionals – doctors, nurses, dentists, and veterinarians. Differences in style or personality mattered very little. We shared the same agony of alcoholism, the same self-loathing, the same regrets and, most of all, the same fears about whether we were going to make it, that is, whether we could stay sober.

Most of the women I met on that first day would be gone in three months at the most. In fact, everyone who came to live in that house stayed for no more than three months – except me.

I honestly don't know if I would have voluntarily stopped drinking. I doubt it. Only force got me into rehab. But, once there, another force started to make itself known, the same force I felt when Jim and I sat in silence the night before I left: the force of love. And that has made all the difference since.

Our home was simple, but we had everything we needed. There were three bedrooms, two bathrooms, a kitchen and a living area. We took turns making the meals and cleaning the house. When we were not busy in the treatment program, we often sat on the patio and just talked about big things, like what alcohol had done to our lives and little things, like what we'd love to have for dinner over the weekend.

It was during one of the morning patio gatherings that I first spotted her. She was emaciated, missing large chunks of hair and had pus coming from her eyes. When I asked one of the women where the golden-haired, small dog came from, she said, "Oh, she is just a stray in the neighborhood. Don't go near her. She probably has all kinds of diseases."

I had never been an ardent animal lover, but I was drawn to this dog. I went over to take a closer look at her and when she looked up at me, I saw in her eyes the same despair and pain that I was feeling. I reached down to pet her and felt a powerful connection with her. Intuitively, I knew that this forlorn, sick animal and I would heal together. Behind those sad eyes, I knew there were vibrant, loving eyes just as I felt my eyes must look like underneath my pain. I felt a love for this dog unlike anything I had ever felt before. The faintest glimmer of hope came over me and, in that moment, Skippy and I started our journey together.

I was not quite sure what to expect at this rehabilitation center, as not all rehab centers are the same. It did not take long to realize that this one would keep me very busy with many required activities including group therapy, individual therapy, homework assignments and attendance at AA meetings. The one good thing about this hectic schedule was that time appeared to pass very quickly and another good thing was that despite all the activities, I still had time to spend with Skippy.

I think she sensed how much I wanted to help her. She waited for me day and night. I started to do everything I could to help her. I fed her healthy meals and gave her baths. Most of all, I gave her my love.

Skippy responded by pouring love into me, and for once in my life, I did not fight it. I began to accept that I was loved, no matter what terrible mistakes I had made in life. To Skippy, it did not matter that I was a hard core alcoholic, perhaps even beyond hope in some people's eyes. When I came home from the therapy sessions, there she was on the steps wagging her tail and jumping for joy. If I left the property to go grocery shopping with the other women, she ran to greet me upon my return and covered me with kisses. I hugged her and told her how much I loved her. Deep down, I was as joyous as she was to be loved.

During the first few months, I became friends with one of the women who had just completed her treatment program at the rehabilitation center. She was a veterinarian and had just returned to work after her time at the center. She watched Skippy and I grow and heal together. I knew

Skippy was getting much better, but I also knew the importance of having a veterinarian examine her.

Heidi offered to see Skippy in her office and do a complete check-up. When all of the tests were completed, Heidi called me with the results. I knew immediately from the sound of her voice that things were not good. She said that Skippy had heartworm disease, which had advanced to stage 4. She explained that basically the worms had invaded Skippy's whole body, and rarely did a dog survive when the disease had progressed this far. She also explained that there was a treatment, but was very concerned that Skippy would not survive it.

I listened and then told Heidi that I wanted her to do whatever it took to help Skippy recover from the heartworm disease. The treatment protocol was that Skippy would be injected with a poison that would kill the worms, but the poison would spread throughout the rest of her body as well. She explained that Skippy would get very sick during the month of the treatment protocol.

After I made the decision, I felt sick. I was so worried that I had made the wrong decision. I was worried that Skippy would die. However, as the days passed, I knew intuitively that this was the right thing to do. I was determined to be with Skippy throughout the ordeal that was ahead. The day Skippy started the treatment was the start of the longest, most difficult month of my life.

Skippy was kept in a cage at the veterinary office. I arrived early each morning, crawled into the cage and held her in my arms. In the beginning, she was so weak that she could barely lift her head. I looked into those beautiful brown eyes of hers and told her how much I loved her. I assured her that I would never leave her. In my heart, I knew she understood me. I stayed with her all day. At the end of the day, the office assistant would have to ask me to leave as it was time to close the office. It was so hard to leave Skippy each day, but I assured her that I would be back in the morning, and every morning, I came back.

I did this for two and a half weeks, and during this time, there were many days that Heidi thought Skippy would not make it. It tore at my heart to watch her. She was so weak that she did not seem able to even open her eyes. She laid in my arms totally listless, but after a few minutes, she would open her eyes and I saw all her courage and all the love she felt for me.

It was during the third week of this long ordeal that for a split second I saw Skippy's tail wag. At first, I thought I was imagining it. I looked down and hoped, really hoped that it would happen again. And it did. Skippy wagged her tail a second time and then a third. I called out for Heidi who ran in and immediately took Skippy's blood pressure. Sure enough, it was finally stable. I could not hold back the tears of joy and relief. "My girl, Skippy" had pulled through! It was a miracle. And I realized that the same could be said for me.

At this point, Skippy and I had become inseparable and our healing journeys were now completely intertwined. As I continued to heal emotionally and physically, so did Skippy. Two weeks after she wagged her tail, she sauntered out of the vet's office and came back to the center with me.

Every day she walked with me to my meetings and lay in the courtyard until it was time to walk home together. She slept in my room at night. Her hair grew in. Her eyes improved. Now she was a most beautiful dog with a full shiny coat, the most expressive brown eyes and the sweetest, loving disposition. Most people could not believe that she was the same dog!

All during this time, Skippy's "owner" was living four houses away. Tex's idea of taking care of a dog was to throw table scraps out into the yard when he thought of it. His yard was an unbelievable mess. The grass was overgrown, there were many dying shrubs, and the front yard was full of garbage, including pizza boxes and more beer cans than I could count. He drove an old, beat up pick-up truck with no caution, whipping around the corners as fast as he could. He knew that I was the person responsible for Skippy's dramatic change, but he still displayed little interest in Skippy or her welfare.

By this time, I had been at the rehab center for nine months, way beyond the average length of stay at a rehab. At this point, my counselor began to discuss the possibility of going home. I supposed I should have been happy, but all I felt was fear.

This treatment center had become such a safe environment and I was not sure that I was ready to go back to the real world. So my counselor recommended that I approach going home in a step by step fashion, and encouraged me to first return home for one weekend only.

Jim and I had a good weekend, but it felt like we were both walking on eggshells. He was so afraid I would drink and was not quite sure how to relate to me. I was not sure how to act either. I also knew that the alcohol store was only minutes away, so the weekend was tense. However, I considered it a success because I stayed sober.

My counselor also considered it a success and felt it was time for me to begin to make serious plans to return home to my life in Reston. She and I also had a heartfelt discussion about Skippy and me. I told her that I simply could not return home without Skippy, and she agreed. She said that she was sure Skippy and I were meant to be together for the rest of our lives. So the next day, I called United Airlines and booked flights for Skippy and me to return home to Virginia.

I was given another weekend pass before returning home, this time to visit my parents who lived a couple of hours drive away. When I left for this visit, I gave the women clear and very detailed instructions about how to take care of Skippy. Even my sister, Maryanne, who lived in Australia and was in touch with me regularly, was eager to make sure that Skippy would be ok while I was away.

I was sad to leave Skippy. Even though I was confident that everything would be okay, I was still sad. When I returned to the center two days later, I did not even bother to bring my bags in. I just ran around to the back yard looking for Skippy, but all I could see were the women sitting on the patio looking very serious. When I noticed that Skippy was not there, I immediately sensed that something was wrong. I asked where Skippy was and no one answered. I felt my heart stop. Inside I was screaming "NO"! I cried out, "Where is Skippy?" One of the women spoke up and said, "She's gone." For a split second, I felt absolutely terrified and screamed, "What do you mean she's gone?"

Before anyone had a chance to reply, my mind jumped back to a moment two weeks before when Tex had yelled from his battered, beer bottle laden truck to one of the women, "You're not doing a bad job taking care of that damn dog, are you? I think I might just take that dog back home with me."

Within a second, I found out that my worst fear had come true. The night before I came home, the women forgot to bring Skippy in. She left the backyard and wandered the neighborhood. Tex saw her, grabbed her, took her back to his house and locked her inside.

Never in my life, before or since, have I felt such desperation. My Skippy was gone! She and I had brought each other back to life, and now we were separated, maybe even forever.

Immediately I ran to Tex's house and saw Skippy through his window. Her paws were up on the window pane as she stared out at me. I ran all around the house. No one was home. Everything was locked tight.

How could this have happened? Skippy and I were scheduled to leave in forty-eight hours to fly home together to Virginia! I had no idea if Skippy would be with me on that flight and I felt utterly helpless. To stand outside, staring at Skippy through the window, locked in and looking so forlorn, was pain that I did not think I could bear.

An eternity seemed to pass while I waited for Tex to pull into his driveway. He was a very tall man and I walked right up to him, looked up, trying to hide my desperation and asked him what was going on.

He explained that Skippy looked "darn good" and he wanted her back. I stared at him in disbelief and tried to hide my trembling lips. How could he forget that I had taken care of Skippy, that I nursed her back to health over the last nine months, while he had completely abandoned her?

Out of nowhere I heard myself telling Tex that I was returning home to Virginia in two days and wanted to take

Skippy with me. He answered, "Well it sure looks like that dog is goin' nowhere. She's mine now and you will never get her back." I turned around and walked back home in shock.

When I got back to the house, I fell on my bed and sobbed, for me and for Skippy. I could not see any way that Skippy would be me in my life again. All I could do was pray that God would somehow see me through this nightmare because I knew Skippy and I belonged together.

A moment later, I heard the phone ring in the living room. My roommate, Bobbie, came to tell me that Maryanne was on the phone from Australia. I said to tell her that I had gone to bed, hoping she would not realize that it was only 4:30 in the afternoon. I could not face telling Maryanne because she would have been heart-broken.

When Bobbie told her this, she immediately knew something was wrong and begged Bobbie to tell her the truth. Reluctantly, Bobbie told her what had happened. Maryanne was shaken, but immediately knew that the best thing to do was enlist the help of friends. She called and emailed as many friends as she could, asking them to pray. In the meantime, everyone at the rehab center, including the staff, were also praying. I needed every one of these prayers because I needed a miracle.

When the tears subsided, I decided that my only hope was to offer Tex money for Skippy. I just had to believe that money would talk! So I went to his house and knocked. When he opened the door, I saw Skippy in the living room. When she saw me, she tried to push past Tex to get to me. He then kicked her and sent her flying back into the room. I watched this in horror and thought I would scream, but knew that I had to do my best and hold it together.

I calmly stated to Tex that I was willing to pay him whatever he wanted. He told me that no money in the world would make him change his mind. Skippy was staying with him! I looked him in the eyes and wanted to scream, "You bastard!" Instead, I turned around and walked away.

I felt total despair. I was supposed to be on the plane in little more than a day. Should I accept that I would go home without Skippy? Everything inside me knew that was wrong.

I could not eat and certainly could not sleep, but somehow I managed to pull it together the next morning and walk to the main courtyard where everyone was gathered. Everyone, including all of the staff, was focused on what had happened the day before.

Two men, who were also in rehab, approached me with an idea about how to get Skippy back. They were willing to break into Tex's house to get Skippy. For a brief moment, I almost agreed to their plan, but knew that in the end, it was not an option.

Another women suggested I show Tex the vet bill and hope that when he saw it, he would be moved enough to give Skippy back. I jumped at this idea, ran to Tex's house and showed him the bill. He didn't budge.

So many people were desperately trying to figure out a way to return Skippy to me, but each idea seemed to go nowhere. Maryanne was calling around the clock with suggestions, but again, none of them held much hope.

Time was running out. I went back to my room and started packing. I was totally numb. I don't even know how I functioned. I had a fleeting thought that maybe I should just call the airline and cancel Skippy's reservation, but I just couldn't do it.

I just had to see Skippy one more time. I put on my shoes and walked straight to Tex's house. I noticed that his truck was not in his driveway. As I approached his house, I thought I was hallucinating. Skippy was outside in the backyard! My heart was pounding. Maybe, just maybe.... I ran to Skippy as fast as I could. She ran to me as fast as she could. All we wanted was to be together again. But we couldn't. There was a fence between us.

I went back to my house, got in the car and drove right back to Tex's. There was a huge barrel pushed up against the door to the fence. When I pushed on the door, nothing budged. I stepped back and then, with everything in me, I ran as hard as I could towards the gate and pushed it with all my might. Then the miracle happened. The gate opened a few inches, just enough for Skippy to get through.

I screamed, "Come on Skippy. We've got to get out of here NOW." The car was running and the doors were open. Skippy jumped into the back seat and I drove away as fast as I could. Tears were pouring down my face and they mingled with all the kisses that Skippy was giving me from the back seat.

I kept driving but was not sure where to go. I knew I could not bring Skippy back to the house because Tex would find her. In a flash I thought of what to do: bring Skippy back to the vet's office.

It was about an hour drive. Skippy continued to give me kisses and her tail never stopped wagging. I was laughing and crying the whole way there. When I brought her in the door to Heidi's office, the entire staff ran to me. They were hugging Skippy and asking a million questions.

Heidi came out of her office and just stared in disbelief. I looked up at her and asked, "Will you help me?" I did not have to wait for an answer. Heidi took over. She knew what time I was leaving the next morning and also knew that I could not bring Skippy back to the house with me. She arranged for Skippy to spend the night at her assistant's house, and for me to pick her up at 4 am on my way to the airport. I loved her plan and left Skippy with her.

On my way home, I finally started to relax and believe that the miracle I asked for had happened. When I drove up my street, I saw lots of people in my front yard and a police car with lights flashing in the driveway. Immediately, I knew there was trouble. All the ease and happiness started to fall away.

I got out of the car and two tall policemen walked straight toward me. They asked me my name and then asked me if I had Skippy. Out of the corner of my eye, I saw Tex standing in the crowd glaring at me. I answered the police, "I don't have a dog."

The police searched my house. Fortunately, Skippy's bowl, leash and toys had all been packed, so there was no sign that a dog had been there. They continued to ask questions and I just kept repeating, "I don't have a dog." Finally, I looked at them and said, "How can I give you a dog when I don't have a dog?"

How the attorney for the rehabilitation center happened to arrive at just that moment, I will never know. The attorney got out of his car, came up to me and asked if I had Skippy. I kept repeating, "I don't have a dog." He asked me to talk with him privately. He looked me in the eye and asked again, "Do you have this dog?"

I had no idea whether I should tell him the truth or not. He could have easily turned me in. I decided to tell him that Skippy was at the vet's office. He listened and walked back to the police. I had no idea what he was going to say to them. He said only one sentence, "She obviously does not have the dog."

Meanwhile, Tex remained furious and continued to accuse me of all sorts of things. This went on for over an hour. In the middle of this, our house phone rang and Bobbie ran in to answer it. It was Maryanne. Bobbie told her the story. Maryanne was not surprised to hear the news. She has an amazing sense of intuition and knew that I was in trouble and needed help. When Bobbie came out and told me that Maryanne called, an amazing calm came over me. I felt that somehow things would be okay.

The police went to the car for what seemed like an eternity. When they came back, they charged me with a misdemeanor. They called me aside and quietly said that if I ever came back to the state of Florida, to make sure that I do not even get a parking ticket. If I did, I could go to jail.

I could not even worry about "being wanted" in the State of Florida. All I could feel was a glimmer of hope that Skippy and I would be together. I called Maryanne and told her about the state of calm that had come over me. She assured me that she had not stopped praying for the last twenty-four hours.

I walked over to the main building to say goodbye. When I entered the courtyard, it seemed that absolutely everyone was there cheering. People were hugging me and giving me words of encouragement. My counselor stood in the background and waited for her turn. She gave me the strongest hug and whispered in my ear, "You and Skippy belong together. Now go home and take good care of her. This has truly been a miraculous healing for both of you." We both had tears in our eyes.

I waved goodbye to everyone and seemed to float back home. The sun was shining and as I looked up into the sky, I said, 'Thank you, God, for this miracle."

I could not sleep that night. I got up at 3 am, put my last few things in the car and drove to pick up Skippy. When I got there at 4 am, she was beside herself with excitement. I put her in the car and took off.

The sun came up as we traveled along the highway together. I don't know if I had ever felt such joy. I knew that this was a new beginning for Skippy and me. We met at a time when we were both utterly desolate. Now we were both happy and at peace.

CHAPTER SIXTEEN

Jim met me at the airport and immediately commented on how well I looked. When I left for Tampa, I was very thin as the drinking had taken a toll on me physically. Now I had gained weight, was tanned from the Florida sunshine and my bright blue eyes were shining again. I loved the compliment, but was much more interested in getting over to the cargo area to pick up Skippy.

Putting her in the crate was difficult, so I was eager to see that she was okay. When I opened the crate, though, she amazed me. She trotted out with her head held high like a prancing racehorse, and her tail wagging at a pace that made me cross-eyed. I hugged her and told her that we were finally home and I believe she understood me.

In the car, Skippy placed her paws on the console and looked back and forth between Jim and me with the precision of someone watching Wimbledon. When she walked into the house, she ran from room to room like a curious three-year-old. That night she fell into a deep sleep at the bottom of our bed, where she would sleep every night for the rest of her life.

Skippy loved Jim, but I had become the center of her world. So it was a gift that the Dentistry Board did not want me to go back to work right away, as it would have been hard for Skippy and I both if I were gone all day.

During this time, I faced the fact that I did not want to go back to dentistry. Not because I didn't enjoy the patients, but because I had a lot of pain in my neck and shoulders. I knew that practicing dentistry would make it worse, and two doctors confirmed that resuming work would only exacerbate the problem. It was time to retire and thanks to Carol's incredible diligence and care during my absence, I knew I could sell the practice for a good price.

It was both an easy decision and a hard one. I loved my patients and I loved dentistry, but I also wanted a break from its demands. I welcomed the opportunity for a more leisurely life, spending time with Jim, spending time with Skippy, going to AA meetings and maybe even developing some other interests.

Two months after the For Sale sign went up, the practice was sold to a woman whom I felt would continue to provide high-quality care to my patients. I received over two hundred letters from patients, congratulating me on my retirement and wishing me well. What touched me the most were the many who said they would miss me. Imagine that, missing your dentist! But they said it and I felt their sincerity.

I loved retirement! I took Skippy to the dog park every day. I made a lot of friends there and after a short time, it was obvious that going there was as beneficial for me as it was for Skippy. I also went to an AA meeting every day and often went out to lunch with my AA friends. I began taking art lessons from my cousin, Jody, who lived in New Hampshire but came to Virginia every six months. I fell in love with painting and before long was working on my first major project: a picture of our childhood home, 239 Oak Ridge Avenue, Summit New Jersey.

Through the art lessons, I developed a deep friendship with Jody, who loved to reminisce about our times with Grandma in New Hampshire. Over time, I received more and more requests to paint other homes and my dining room took on the look of an art studio, with paints and canvases everywhere. Jody had given me a great gift: the ability to create something beautiful all by myself. None of this, though, could have happened without my sobriety.

CHAPTER SEVENTEEN

It was a sunny day and I was happily painting when the phone rang at 12 noon on July 5, 2004. It was my brother, Rick. He was upset, on the verge of tears, but I could still hear his words and they made my heart stop.

"Mom's had a massive stroke. It doesn't look good." He tried to continue but he was just too close to tears to be intelligible. He put Dad on the phone who was in worse shape than Rick. Then I began to sob, crying out, "Is she okay?" Finally, Rick's wife, Lynn, got on the phone and with a calm and strong voice, she was able to communicate what had happened.

She confirmed that Mom had a massive stroke about one hour before. The doctors were running tests to see is she was a candidate for a specific drug named TPA that might minimize the effects of the stroke. If so, it would greatly improve her prognosis. I had trouble taking all of this in, but was able to clearly state, "I can pack and be on the road in twenty minutes. Where is the hospital?"

After Lynn gave me the directions, I turned to Jim and said simply, "I've got to go". I threw some clothes in my suitcase, grabbed Skippy and her things and started the four-hour drive to New Jersey.

The ride that I had made so many times and so easily in the past was now unbearable. Each minute seemed so long and filled with anxiety. All I could imagine was that I would arrive only to learn that Mom had died.

When I arrived at the hospital, Dad, Rick and Lynn were in the waiting area, each looking dazed. Rick explained that our mother was able to have the drug, TPA, which would minimize the effects of the stroke. Our deepest hope was that she would still be able to move and talk.

A few moments later, the four of us entered the room. Mom was very still, very pale and her eyes were closed. I spoke to her softly and she opened her eyes. She looked back and forth at the four of us with a confused look. She did not say a word and we did not know if she could.

Dad spoke to her explaining that she had a stroke. Her eyes opened wide. Clearly the news agitated her, but it seemed as though she could not speak. At this point, all I could do was turn my head as the tears streamed down my face. Rick spoke next and told Mom that the doctors felt she would be okay. He reached for her hand, held it in his and asked if she could move her fingers. Four sets of eyes stared at her hand with the greatest of intensity. Nothing happened. Rick then gently lifted the sheet off Mom's feet and asked her to try to move her toes. It took at least twenty seconds but finally it happened. Mom was able to move her toes. This was the sign we were praying for, the sign that indicated that she might recover.

After awhile, Dad went home. At 85, the intensity of the day had taken a toll on him. After the nurse asked the rest of us to leave, we stood in the parking lot together and finally let ourselves feel the heartbreak and acknowledge all the unanswered questions.

Andrew was out of the country on business. When he learned the news, he got on the first flight home. Maryanne, in Australia, wanted to return immediately, but we advised her to wait until we knew more from the doctors.

The next morning the four of us arrived at the hospital to hear the doctors tell us that it was too early to assess what damage the stroke had done. It would take time, perhaps a lot, to know any more. We became very good at waiting.

After four or five days, Mom tried to speak. It was difficult to understand her, but each day she improved. She started moving her right arm and leg fairly easily, but she still had a lot of trouble coordinating the movements on the left side of her body. Her left side was not paralyzed, but we could tell that she would have to re-learn how to use it.

After two weeks, Mom was moved to a stroke rehabilitation center. We were all encouraged by her improvement, but knew there was a long way to go. Andrew was coming to New Jersey often and, at this point, Maryanne was on her way from Australia.

Maryanne and I stayed at Dad's home in Spring Lake and together worked out a daily routine. In the morning we did errands, buying whatever Mom needed. In the afternoon, after she finished physical therapy, we arrived at the center bearing gifts and treats ready to spend the next seven or eight hours with her.

One might think these were sad times, but they were not. Mom and Maryanne and I spent much of this time laughing together, and sometimes laughing so hard that our stomachs hurt. Just when we thought we could not take another minute of the pain of such hysterical laughing, one of us would tell another story from the past and the laughing would start all over again. We spent almost no time discussing the stroke or Mom's post-stroke status with her. We seemed to know intuitively that what she needed most was laughter and joy, and we were on a mission to provide her with both. We were pleased when one nurse after another came in saying our laughter was contagious, and that it was brightening up the whole ward. These were happy days.

The best part of our visit with Mom was taking her around the grounds of the center in her wheelchair. She loved being outside in the fresh air, feeling the sunshine and the breeze. When we returned, we would go downstairs to buy her an ice cream, which was her favorite food both before and after the stroke! After that, it was time to help her get ready for bed and for her nightly episode of Law and Order. When we turned off the lights at 9:30 each night, we watched Mom struggle to keep her eyes open, so determined to find out who'd done it!

After one month, the day finally came when Mom would return home. In anticipation, Dad had done his usual excellent job of organizing, this time a team of people who would help Mom's recovery, including a physical therapist, a speech therapist and a home attendant. After just one week, Mom was using a walker and walking more steadily each day. Her speech was good as was her spirits. At this point, Dad was diagnosed with spinal stenosis. He was in a lot of pain and had difficulty walking. Between getting Dad to his many doctors' appointments and helping Mom, Maryanne and I did not stop.

Dad often likened Maryanne and me to Mary and Martha from biblical times. Martha was the tireless worker, who never stopped working physically from dawn to dusk. Mary, on the other hand, accomplished works through talking and just being with people.

Maryanne was certainly Mary. She never tired of sitting with Mom and talking with her, practicing her physical therapy exercises, coming up with creative ways to keep her engaged in life, whether it was arranging for her spiritual book club to meet again or discussing current events with her.

I, on the other hand, was Martha. I never stopped moving. If I was not making lists of grocery store items, I was at the store buying them. Any errand that needed to be done, I did it. I also quickly became Dad's chauffeur as it was difficult for him to drive. Several times a week, Dad and I traveled to his various doctors' appointments together.

With the combined efforts of Martha and Mary, along with the constant support of my brothers and sisters-in-law and the kindness of my parents' many friends, the Spring Lake house by the sea began to come alive again, absorbing the brightening energy of a summer at the Jersey shore.

My parents' home was perfectly situated to absorb this shore energy. It was not right on the ocean, but "one back." It was seated at a remarkable angle across from the ocean, giving the upstairs master bedroom a stunning panoramic view of the boardwalk from its balcony, as well as a view of the beach-goers from the porch below. It was here on the porch where Mom spent much of her time relaxing, watching the beach-goers and breathing in the sea air.

Skippy was a breath of fresh air in our home during this difficult time, not only for me, but for Mom as well. She would light up every time Skippy entered the room and Skippy looked equally happy to be at Mom's side. She also loved going up to the boardwalk and running on the beach during the off hours. With Skippy in our lives, life seemed to have just a touch of normalcy.

On a sunny day at the end of the summer, Mom and I sat relaxing together on the porch. After Maryanne ran to get her camera to take a photo of us, Mom asked me to come and sit closer to her. When I did, she spoke softly but strongly, "This has been a hard time for all of us. I have seen how strong you are and that you have been able to stay sober. I want you to know how proud I am of you."

Tears welled up in her eyes as she reached for my hand.

"It's everything I have prayed for, Patsy. I now know that I can go in peace."

I did not know what to say. I simply held Mom's hand tightly, confirming through touch what her words meant to me. And I knew that I would cherish that moment forever.

By the middle of September, Mom had recovered faster than anyone anticipated. There was still room for improvement, but all the therapists were optimistic that she would make a complete recovery.

I sat back and watched the power of love heal our mother. Both Andrew and Jim came up from Washington on the weekends. Rick and Lynn, who were with us in Spring Lake, were devoted to spending time with Mom, often stopping by several times a day. Mom's countenance brightened when her visitors arrived, particularly when any of her four grandchildren walked into the room. All embarrassment about her stroke-related liabilities would vanish; she was simply thrilled to be with the people she loved.

Jim was always loving and supportive during this time. He never complained about my being away from home. In fact, he always assured me that it was important that I be with Mom. On the weekends when he came to Spring Lake, I fell into his arms exhausted but also grateful that he was there with me. Jim has an incredible ability to be fully supportive without drawing any attention to himself in the process. I was able to draw on all his love and support and feel renewed after every visit.

Maryanne stayed in New Jersey two months helping Mom recover. She and I had loved helping our mother and were so happy to see her life returning to normal, yet it was time for Maryanne to go home to her family in Australia.

When we said goodbye at the airport, Maryanne hesitated at the glass doors looking as though she could not walk through them. Sadly she did, and I drove the two hours back to a house that felt very different. Mom and Dad and I ate dinner together, not saying very much. After I tucked Mom into bed, I cried myself to sleep.

The sun shone brightly the next day, perhaps knowing that we really needed its light and warmth. The three of us looked forward to a number of visitors who would be dropping in to celebrate Labor Day.

After the holiday weekend, Rick and Lynn moved back to northern New Jersey in time for their youngest son, Michael, to begin his senior year in high school. Rick and Lynn had planned a 2-weeek trip to Europe and asked if I could drive up to their home in the evenings to be with Michael, and then go back to the shore the next day. I was happy to do it and was able to keep up the daily schedule with Mom.

After wishing them bon voyage, I drove down to Spring Lake in time to greet Mom's physical therapist. Though she did not know it, this was an important physical therapy session that I did not want to miss.

For the three weeks prior to this session, Mom's physical therapy session included a "walk" to the beach. Holding her walker, with Dave the therapist on one side and me on the other, Mom would walk the half block to the road, cross it and then walk up to the boardwalk. Here she would gaze upon the ocean that she loved so much. The whole process took about a half-hour, required tremendous focus, and brought Mom so much joy. On this particular day, things would be very different.

When Dave arrived, he wasted no time in telling Mom what the day held in store for her.

"Rita, we are going to do something new today. When you get to the boardwalk, I am going to take the walker from you so that you can walk by yourself on the boardwalk, holding onto the rail."

Mom looked excited and frightened at the same time. She claimed she did not think she could do it, but I knew my mother and did not believe her claim. She would try hard and do her best, as she always did.

When the moment came to shed the walker, there was no doubt or fear in her face. She looked completely focused, unaware of Dave or me. After a few steps, though, she looked up at me and exclaimed, "Look, Patsy, I'm walking!"

I had never seen such a smile on Mom's face in all my life. She was absolutely beaming. I took photo after photo so that Maryanne, Rick and Andrew could share in her joy. After the photos, she asked if I knew this was going to happen. I just smiled and hugged her.

At home, she was quick to place a call to her sister in New Hampshire to share the news. While she chatted enthusiastically, clearly excited about the full recovery ahead, I got ready to go and spend the evening with my nephew. I blew her a kiss and sailed out the door, so happy about the day.

The next morning, Dave was due to arrive at eleven and Mom and I both expected another solo walk on the boardwalk. When the doorbell rang, I met Dave, excited to share all the happiness of the afternoon and evening before. In mid-sentence, I heard a crash from the porch. Dave and I raced to see what had happened. We found my mother lying on the floor with a heavy wrought iron chair lying on its side next to her. Horrified, I bent down to her pleading for reassurance that she was okay. She seemed shaken, but was able to tell me that she was so excited when she heard Dave at the door that, without thinking, she tried to get up and greet him. Dave asked a number of more clinical questions trying to assess the damage. Dad was right there also, obviously upset. He too was intent on discovering the extent of the damage. Mom was able to tell us that her left side was hurting but other than that she felt okay.

Dave asked me to come into the living room where he told me quietly that he felt she might have broken a rib. He said it would be wise to get her to Urgent Care, about two miles away. No one spoke in the car. We were shocked and overwhelmed, wondering how it was possible to move from elation to heartbreak so quickly. When I told the receptionist at Urgent Care what had happened, Mom was quickly ushered into the x-ray room. A half-hour later, we had the news. Mom had broken seven ribs. The doctor's prescription was complete bed rest and painkillers, advising us that it would take two to three months for the ribs to heal.

Mom laid on the gurney utterly still. She was pale and very weak, but most of all she seemed in great pain, so much so that she dare not move. With the help of a male nurse, we got her into the car and propped many blankets and pillows around her to ease the pain. I drove as slowly as I could so the car would remain steady. Despite my efforts, Mom winced in pain with every bump and I thought my heart would break listening to her cries. When we arrived home, we needed the help of a neighbor to get her inside and into bed. I quickly went to the pharmacy, got Mom's pain medication and gave it to her. By this time, she was writhing in pain whenever she moved.

Dad was ashen when I said goodbye to him to drive up north to stay with my nephew. I was almost as frightened for him as I was for Mom. The hour-long drive was awful. If emotional pain can be equated with physical pain, I believed Mom and I were in the same depth of pain.

"My God, Patsy, are you okay?"

I could not even respond to Michael's question. I just fell to the floor sobbing. Michael sat next to me and put his arm around me. As I was able to speak, I told him what had happened to his Nana. Michael listened and said very little while he kept his arms around me.

We ate dinner but neither of us could say much. We just wanted the phone to ring with good news. Finally the phone did ring, but we did not receive the good news we wanted.

Dad was fighting back tears, but was able to explain.

"It's not good. After you left, I checked on Mom and she did not wake up. I assumed she had passed out from the pain. I called 911 and she went to the hospital by ambulance.

She had more x-rays there and one clearly showed that one of her broken ribs had punctured a lung. She had lost quite a lot of blood before she even arrived at the hospital."

At a certain point, Dad could not continue. He was able to state the facts, but could no longer hold back his feelings.

"My God, Patsy, we may lose her."

I heard his words, but had no reply. All we could do was rest in the heartbreak together.

Instinctively I told him that he must go to bed and get as much rest as he could. I assured him that I would be there early in the morning to take him to the hospital.

As soon as our call was finished, the phone rang again and then again. Rick was calling from Italy and Maryanne was calling from Australia. Both wanted many more details than I could give, and both wanted to know if they should come home. I told them not to get on a plane until I learned more the next day.

I tried to follow the advice I gave Dad, but I could not sleep. I just wanted to get to Spring Lake. I wanted to see my mother.

I gasped when I saw her in Intensive Care - so many tubes and machines, with an assigned nurse focused solely on her care. I could not believe this was my mother who had been triumphantly awaiting her walk on the boardwalk only twenty four hours before.

Dad and I sat down in the two chairs beside Mom's bed. The shock began to wear off and Dad started to cry. Through his tears, he called out to her, "Rita, please don't leave me. I love you so much."

Then he turned to me and asked if we could pray together and we did, through our tears.

Finally, the doctor came in and explained that there had been so much internal bleeding that it was not clear that Mom would survive. Dad's face turned ashen. As soon as I could, I convinced him to go home. I was scared I was going to lose them both!

After Dad left, I sat with Mom who remained motionless. I began to talk to her and I did not stop talking for hours. I did not know if should could hear me and I did not care. I wanted her to know how much I loved her and how much I wanted her to stay with me, with all of us. Then I recited mine and her favorite prayers. The hours flew by, but nothing changed. Mom remained motionless and appeared on the verge of death.

The next morning, when Dad and I arrived at the hospital, the doctors met us with sobering news. Mom could not breathe on her own. Her body was too exhausted and the effort of breathing was weakening her by the minute. They wanted permission to place her on a ventilator, a machine that would essentially breathe for her.

Dad did not hesitate to give this permission. It was agonizing to think of Mom struggling to breathe. We welcomed the news of the ventilator, both for her sake and our own.

Mom did look better on the ventilator, not so exhausted and not so ashen. Despite this apparent relief, she appeared to be in a deep sleep most of the time. Occasionally, she opened her eyes and we could tell she recognized us. Even more occasionally, she became animated during these moments. Dad spoke and tried to reassure her that she was going to get well, but he seemed to be reassuring himself as much as he was Mom. The truth was we simply did not know what the future held for her.

Once or twice when I was sitting with Mom, she opened her eyes, looked right into mine and smiled. In these moments, all heartbreak vanished. I simply rested in the love that Mom and I had for each other, a love that I knew would last for eternity.

CHAPTER EIGHTEEN

It had been two weeks since the fall. Rick and Lynn had returned home from their trip. Andrew arrived from Washington and Maryanne was on her way back from Australia. At this point, the doctors wanted to discuss Mom's prognosis with the family.

Dad, representing all of us, had a big decision to make. The damage to Mom's lungs was extensive and the respite of the ventilator had not resulted in greater healing of this damage. The doctors felt that unless she had surgery to repair the damage, she would not survive. On the other hand, there was a significant risk that she would not survive the surgery. But Dad did not hesitate in the face of this nightmarish decision. He asked the doctors to perform the surgery as soon as possible.

Dad and I waited at home during the surgery, though we could not be in the same room. Individually, the pain was great, but when we were together, it seemed unbearable. I kept busy around the house while Dad read every word of the newspaper. Actually, I think he read every word twice.

Finally, the silent tension was broken by the sound of the phone. I held my breath while Dad answered and listened intently. I could tell how hard he was trying to stay strong.

A few moments, later he turned to me and said, "She almost died on the operating table, but she made it. The next 24 hours are critical, but the lung is repaired." I was ecstatic! Yes, the news was still frightening, but Mom was alive. And I knew how much she would fight to stay that way.

It was not an easy time for anyone in the family. Still, the value that Mom held so dear to her heart – the love of family – did shine through. We all wanted to do everything we could to help Mom and Dad through this time.

Mom survived the surgery, but her progress was slow. She did not seem capable of breathing without the ventilator. Countless attempts were made to wean her off the ventilator, but invariably she started gasping for breath and was quite frightened.

Finally, the most painful truth became obvious: Mom would have to live on the ventilator in a nursing home until she could breathe without it. Granted it was a nursing home that did have some success in weaning people off ventilators, but it was still a nursing home.

A few weeks after she moved to the nursing home, the phone rang in the middle of the night and the news was grim. Mom suffered a heart attack and had been rushed to the hospital. The following morning, Dad and I went to see her. Once again I gasped silently when I saw her. She was not only on the ventilator but now was hooked up to an incredible array of tubes, machines and IV's.

A few days later, she was back in the nursing home, a place that I was growing to dislike very much. The staff made promises about the care that they were going to give Mom, but they did not fulfil them. I became angry on several occasions just to have them pay attention to my requests, none of which were even remotely out of line.

The situation was especially upsetting for Dad. He was a man who took pride in handling things well and yet, in this situation, he was rendered virtually powerless. As a result, he became weakened and brittle. I could sense this and so could Mom's sister and oldest friend who came to visit. It became obvious we needed a place other than Dad's home, where people could stay overnight while visiting Mom. I found a 2 bedroom apartment close to the nursing home, I rented it quickly as it seemed critical that Mom be able to see those who had traveled some distance to see her.

On the surface, I was handling things well, but, just like Dad, felt powerless and discouraged. So one night, when my aunt and mother's best friend sat down for their cocktail, I went in the other bedroom and poured mine. The vodka did what it always did – it took the pain away – until the next morning when the shame and guilt replaced the euphoria of the night before. After several days of this pattern, I recognized that this cycle would end in disaster, as it always had. And so when I returned home, I told Jim what happened and worked to get back on track quickly. Plus, I wanted to be ready for cousin Jody's arrival.

Jody was more than a cousin, of course. She was my art teacher and friend. I was so happy to have her stay with Skippy and me in the apartment, and so happy to see her face light up when Jody and Skippy would sail into the room together. This was the one redeeming feature of the nursing home: they allowed me to bring Skippy in every day to see Mom.

Jody has a special gift with those who are ill. She is gentle and loving, but also wonderfully creative. She thought of things to do for Mom that never would have occurred to me. One day, I left for a few hours and when I returned, saw that Jody had fixed Mom's hair; given her a manicure and pedicure; helped her do the post–stroke exercises and had read her several stories! Whatever she did, she did with patience and love. And Mom responded fully to all of this loving care.

A few weeks later, Mom was able to come off the ventilator. It was a day of celebration for us all. Yet her body was very weak and became more so after a number of minor heart attacks. Eventually, she had to go back on the ventilator. She was simply too exhausted to breathe on her own. At this point, the doctors indicated that it was quite likely Mom would never be able to breathe on her own and need to be on a ventilator for the rest of her life.

Mom was always ahead of her time. Many years before, she had asked that Dad draw up a living will for her. She was adamant that she did not want to be kept alive by any artificial means.

Even though Mom made her wishes clear years before, the decision to turn off her ventilator was something that Dad did not want to consider at all. It took him weeks, after learning Mom would probably not survive without the ventilator, before he was ready to even discuss the decision. In the end, it was probably the most agonizing time of his life. He deliberated for weeks, calling his friends who were priests, meeting with them and meeting with the hospital staff, reviewing her living will over and over. He did everything in his power, everything, to ensure that he was making the right decision.

He spoke to each one of us children, making sure we all felt in agreement with the decision he had reached to turn our mother's ventilator off. The decision, he explained, was based on the medical conclusion that Mom could not breathe on her own without the ventilator. In other words, the ventilator was keeping her alive and that this was exactly the situation she did not want to happen.

The ventilator was turned off in early May of 2005. To everyone's surprise, Mom did not die when she was taken off of it. In fact, she perked up, but was still extremely weak. During this time, Maryanne, Rick, Andrew and I all had a chance to see her, be with her and laugh with her one more time.

Mom had always said, or indicated through her nods, that she would attend her only granddaughter, Kristen's, graduation from college in late May 22, 2005. In fact, she even indicated what outfit she wanted to wear. She was determined to be with her granddaughter, one way or the other.

On May 22, 2005 at 12 noon, Mom closed her eyes for the last time and went home to God. Only one day earlier, Kristen walked onto the stage and received her diploma. In her own way, Mom was with Kristen on her Graduation Day.

I ached in a way that I had never ached. I clung tenaciously to the memory of a week before her death when she whispered in my ear, "I love you so much." My mother did love me very much. She loved me through years and years of the nightmare of alcoholism. She never closed her heart to me, no matter how much pain she suffered in the face of my drinking, nor how frustrated she was with her inability to get me to stop.

But she had also loved many, many people and they came out in the hundreds to express their gratitude and to say goodbye. Twenty-three of my twenty-five cousins came from all over the US to be with us. Many of her students, from the past and present, found their way to the Spring Lake church where her funeral Mass was held.

Her students were unhesitating in their praise,

"I loved your mother."

"She was so good to me."

"She was the best teacher I ever had."

"I loved to see what your mother would wear each day. She had such style."

On the morning of her burial, the immediate family was at the funeral home to say a final goodbye. Before the casket was closed, I knelt in front of Mom and placed my AA medallion in the palm of her hand. I felt I could hear her say, "Thank you, sweetheart, I am so proud of you."

I was not prepared for the grief or the intense loneliness that followed. I would often start crying spontaneously and could not stop. One day, the tears came so quickly and so intensely that I had to leave a shopping cart filled with purchases right in the middle of the store aisle.

I cancelled plans often, but the one thing I did not miss were my AA meetings. Many times I just sat in the back of the room and cried, but at least I went. During this time, I often sat quietly next to Skippy and patted her gently as this helped ease the loneliness. I could not ignore that Skippy was struggling herself. She was fourteen now and had many symptoms of old age, including very arthritic legs. I began to carry her up and down the steps many times per day, because she insisted on being near me.

When I brought her to the vet, she explained that there was not one particular thing wrong with Skippy. It was just old age. She told me to watch her and if she stopped eating or drinking to call her right away.

Just as the vet had said, Skippy did stop eating and drinking. With an aching heart, I called the vet who asked me to bring Skippy in at 4 p.m. that day. After the call, I just lay next to Skippy on the floor wondering how I would survive the next loss.

Skippy was near death and she knew it, yet she still poured her love out to me. Her deep brown eyes conveyed the depth of feeling they offered right from start of our earliest days together. Tears poured down my face as I felt the wound of love, this very wound that had almost broken me in my lifetime was now healing me. I did not hold back the tears nor try to protect myself from this pain. I yielded and allowed **love to finally triumph in my life** as my darling Skippy died in my arms.

I don't know where I found the strength to get through the next few months, but I was given just enough to put one foot ahead of the other each day. Of course, it helped that Maryanne was visiting me and we were planning to go to Spring Lake together.

We went to Spring Lake to be with our father and to go through Mom's belongings. While taking one glorious outfit after another out of the closet, remembering how she looked when she wore them, remembering the many stories from Mom's magnificent life, we laughed ourselves to tears. We cried too, in the realization that she would never light up a room with her stunning outfits again.

Dad took us out for dinner just as he always had, and the memories of our glorious nights as a family in New York and Atlantic City came back as if they had only happened yesterday.

After one month, Maryanne flew back to Australia and I went back to Virginia, where I knew the greatest challenge awaited me. I learned from the past that once an alcoholic gets through a crisis, that the next weeks and months can be a slippery ride. Once the challenge of withstanding the crisis was over, the alcoholic can begin to feel it is safe to have a drink or two. I knew I had to be careful.

I made sure I got to an AA meeting every day. I had grown to love the friendship I developed through the years with this group. I did not have to prove anything. Quite the opposite, I had already "proven" just how low I could go when I was drinking. Now each day of sobriety was an achievement all its own.

I decided I needed a hobby and I chose gardening. I did not know the difference between a flower and a weed when I started, so I read and read until I was knowledgeable at least "on paper." But I had to get my hands dirty and once I did, I could not stop. I pulled weeds, weeds and more weeds until I had a large patch just waiting for color and beauty.

Pink azaleas, white azaleas and purple azaleas (I like azaleas!) covered the patch and were surrounded by rhododendra of every color imaginable. Bright round hydrangeas completed the orchestra of color. But my garden was not actually finished. I needed it to convey signs of my healing and remembrance of those whose love has helped me heal.

I took my inspiration from the boardwalk of Spring Lake, where every few meters one could sit on a bench with a plaque on it, a plaque dedicated in someone's memory. At home in Reston, my bench was black wrought iron and was surrounded by the bright pinks and purples of my flowers.

A gray stone path was carefully placed in an inviting way leading up to the bench. Then, on the bench itself were two plaques that read:

"In loving memory of Mom. Twas heaven here with you."

"In loving memory of Skippy. We found each other."

The garden needed its finishing touch, which was a large rock painted white with the word "Serenity" stenciled on it in blue. Mom and Skippy believed that one day I could enjoy serenity, even when I could not begin to imagine it. I will be grateful to them forever.

Between AA meetings, gardening and painting, my life was full but was missing something: a dog. I had three cats, but I missed having a canine friend, and I suspect the cats did too. So I made an appointment to visit the Fairfax County Animal Shelter the next day.

Walking through the shelter, I wanted to take all the dogs home, but finally decided on a beagle. He seemed very happy to be with me and I thought it would be perfect. In less than an hour, it could not have been more imperfect.

Within seconds of being in the house and off the leash, the dog went wild. He ran around with break neck speed, knocking over a large table whose lamp went flying. He tried to climb up the curtains, but they fell down on top of him. He jumped on to a chair and then on to the dining room table, which he monogrammed with his claws. He had not seen the cats yet, but I knew all my plans of helping them "to get to know each other" would be futile. I had only one choice – to bring him back to the shelter as soon as possible.

"I hope you understand that you will not be allowed to adopt from the shelter again."

This was the woman's response to my horrified look and tale. I did not have time to take offense. If I was going to be blackballed by the Animal Shelter, then so be it. Friends came to the rescue, reminding me that I could never have predicted what had happened. They encouraged me to look on the internet, explaining that this was becoming the best way to find a rescue dog.

I did not waste any time. I found websites of the animal shelters in our area and began scrolling. I came upon the picture of a white dog with a sweet yet comical expression, described as half poodle and half Bijon. I called the shelter immediately.

"If you are really serious, I would not waste any time" was the woman's response to my query about this delightful-looking being. I was not sure if she said this about every dog, but I decided not to take any chances. Jim and I drove the hour-long drive to the shelter early the next morning.

When we arrived, our name was first on the list but there were twenty names after ours, confirming that the woman's advice to move quickly was sound. The dog was found under a bench several counties away. It took three washings to discover that he was white. The shelter named him Dior and suggested that we take the newly-named Dior for a walk. We walked for about a half-hour, all over the grounds of the shelter and then sat down on a bench.

Dior seemed to enjoy being with us, but when he sat down, I could tell that it was more than enjoyment. He actually felt very safe. He lay on his back with his four legs straight in the air while Jim, kneeling beside him, rubbed his belly. Within an hour, we knew Dior would join our family and we also knew that Dior would be given a new name. A week later, following an interview at our home with a shelter representative, Murphy came to our home and he has been living happily with us ever since.

It was clear that something was happening in my life, something subtle but powerful. I began to notice that I enjoyed being with people in a way I never had before. Sometimes I felt a spontaneous enjoyment with new friends and sometimes with people I had known a long time. It was as if for the first time in my life I felt worthy of someone's attention and, as a result, I could simply relax and enjoy myself.

One day at an AA meeting, I saw a woman that I had not seen before. I could not stop staring at her because she actually looked just like me. She was my size, had blonde hair, blue eyes and her style was much like mine. After the meeting while walking to our cars, we started to chat and realized we had much in common. We had both gone to Catholic primary and high schools where we were taught by loving nuns. We were in the same class at Georgetown, though we had not crossed paths. And both of our fathers were Georgetown graduates. I was ready and able to enjoy my new friend, Marialice, especially since we had so much in common and looked like sisters. I will always be grateful for the support she has given me through the ups and downs of my recovery.

My newfound enjoyment of people also extends to those I have known for a long time, like Jim's children, Jen and Jason. They have always remained so open-hearted to me over the twenty years I have known them, and of course, it has been my great joy to have their four wonderful children in my life.

Carol and I still talk on the phone every day, twenty-one years after our first day of working together as a dental team and our husbands can't get over it! She traveled with me to New Jersey after my mother died, and has walked with me through every challenge on my road to sobriety. It is hard to put into words how grateful I am for who she is and what she has given me.

My life today is rich with friendship, but also simple. I get up every day at 4:30 so that I can read my AA meditations and pray. One of my favorite readings is from the Daily Reflections, a book of reflections by AA members for AA members:

"Upon entering AA, I listen to others talk about the reality of their drinking: loneliness, terror and pain. As I listened further, I soon heard a description of a very different kind – the reality of sobriety."

It is a reality of freedom and happiness, purpose and direction and the serenity and peace with God, ourselves and others. By attending meetings, I am reintroduced to that reality over and over. I see it in the eyes and hear it in the voices of those around me. By working the program, I find the direction and strength within which to make it mine. The joy of AA is that this new reality is available to me.

Yes, this new reality is available to me, but I must choose it. I must choose it every day, and particularly in every moment when I become restless, irritable and discontented. In order to avoid the abyss of alcoholism, it is not enough to just remember how bad it was when I was drinking. I must also remember that the only thing standing between me and drinking is my spiritual life, my actual living connection to God. AA says that we are not cured of alcoholism. Instead, what we have is a daily reprieve contingent on the maintenance of our spiritual condition. Of this, I have no doubt.

As mentioned before, it never occurred to me to write my story. And I could not have done it without my sister, Maryanne. About a year ago, a friend of hers was writing an anthology of short stories about dogs. She asked Maryanne to be a contributor. Maryanne said yes, but she also volunteered me!

When I heard the news, I did point out the obvious to her: I am not a writer and I don't even know how to type! But Maryanne did not accept the excuses and suggested I start writing the story of my life with Skippy. She encouraged me to write it in long hand and then read it to her over the phone. Maryanne loves editing, so she would edit the story and then read it back to me. I then suggested any changes to her editing. We worked like this, back and forth, to produce my short story and then we worked with like this for a year to produce this book.

Several months after I started writing, my story was published in <u>The Wonderful World of Dogs</u>. I never thought I would be an author and was filled with pride to become one.

I sent copies to many friends, to my brothers and, of course, to my father. A few days after my father received his copy, he called and left a message for me:

"Patsy, thank you for sending me this book. I have read your story three times. It is a wonderful story. You should be very proud of yourself."

EPILOGUE

Ten days later, on March 25th, 2011, my father died peacefully while on a cruise ship. All my life I worked to gain my father's approval and feel his pride in me. When I was not busy doing this, I was upsetting him terribly through my drinking. Now, I am no longer doing either.

Love did triumph in my life. I finally allowed all of the love – from God, Jim, my family and my friends – to pour into me and give me the courage and strength needed to heal.

SECOND EPILOGUE

A few days before this manuscript was going to the publisher, something wonderful happened. I saw John Motley again. I had only seen him for brief moments since our wedding was cancelled twenty-seven years before. I went to his home to deliver some framed pictures, which I found in the back of my closet after all these years. I found myself saying something to John that I knew needed to be said. I thanked him for having the courage to do what he did so many years before. And I told him how much I respected him for his courage.

When I arrived home, I told Jim what I had said to John. He pointed out that I had just completed the Ninth Step of the Twelve Steps of AA, which is to make amends to those who have been affected by one's drinking. Jim told me how proud he was of me and said he hoped I felt proud of myself. And at last, I do.

Patsy and Jim

Patsy's mother and father

Rick, Maryanne, Patsy & Andrew

Patsy and Maryanne

Rick, Patsy & Andrew

Patsy, her mother & Maryanne

Patsy and Skippy

Patsy and Murphy

My mother, Skippy and Me after the stroke

My mother's triumphant walk after her stroke

Patsy and her nephew Peter

Patsy at Maryanne's wedding

Maryanne, Patsy and Rick

Patsy and Maryanne

My Painting of my Childhood home - 2002

My serenity garden – created 2003

Dr. Patricia R. Kentz, DDS was born and raised in Summit, New Jersey. She graduated magna cum laude from Georgetown University in 1976, where she majored in pre-med. In 1980, she graduated from the Georgetown University Dental School with highest honors. She practiced dentistry for twenty four years. Today she devoted her life to her recovery and to helping those in recovery. She lives with her husband, Jim, and their small menagerie in Reston, Virginia. Love's Triumph is her first book. She is presently at work on the screenplay for a movie.